Coding in Style

Coding in Style

by Dragos Ionel

2018

First Printing: 2016
Second Printing: 2018

ISBN 978-1-329-90766-9

www.adelante.ca

Available also in Kindle format at amazon.com

Editing: Dharmendra Chauhan, Florin Lohan, Max Korytko

Cover: Richard Payment (www.richardpayment.com)

Dedication

To all the developers who at least once said,
"Who wrote this piece of junk?"
and then discovered it was themself.

Sharing is caring

So did my kids tought me after starting kindergarten.

If you purchased this book in any format, you are entitled to get, for free, the book in PDF format.

Other than selling it, I'll probably agree for you to use it in pretty much any way you want: print, share, email it. Just send me an email before.

I would be honored if you find the information worth sharing it.

Feel free to drop me a note or request the PDF version at www.adelante.ca.

Contents

Introduction...1

Code standards...3
  Indenting 3
  Line length 4
  Semicolon 5
  Brackets...5
    Round brackets 5
    Curly brackets ("{" and "}").......................................6
  Empty spaces 6
    Equal...6
    Arrays...6
    Function 6
    Variable declaration...7
    Boolean conditions...7
    Comparison...7
    Comma...7
  Empty lines 8

Naming 10
  Introduction..10
  Why is a name important?..10
  Variables and constants 11
    Choose a rule for capitalizing and stick to it.............11
    Names are nouns 12
    Who are you?...12
    No comment needed 12
    Speak English 13
    Be specific...13
    Context...14
    Shortest but no shorter than that................................14
    Never use negations in Boolean values 14
    Unit of measure..15
    Add the types at the end of variable name 15
    Don't be creative..16
    Do not be smarty pants..16
  Functions 17
    Whatcha doin'? 17
    Capitalization 18
    Be specific...18

Long is okay 18
Function parameters 19
   Number of parameters 19
Classes and structures..20
   Use nouns for their names..20
   Capitalization 20
   Be specific..20
   As long as it need 21
   No prefix..21
Types 21
Enumerations..21
Projects 21
Libraries 22
General notes about naming..22
   Avoid ambiguous names 22
   How long is too long..23
   Remove useless words..24
   Worst enemy: misleading names 24

Comments 25
Introduction..25
When to use comments 25
Document "Why" 26
Only if needed 26
Comments are not code..27
Mark code 27
   MARK:..28
   TODO: 29
   FIXME: 29
Document your thoughts 30
Libraries 30
Do not comment junk..31
Comment bigger chunks of code. 32
Keep it short 32
Make it clear and up to date 32
Don't be funny. 32
Don't be an artist 33
Don't track the history 33
Commits 34
Syntax..34
Markup..35
   How to visualize markup in Xcode 35
   Where to add markup code..37

Markup code syntax 37
Special commands 39

Coding with grace 43
Introduction 43
Variables and constants 43
  Types 43
  Location for constants 44
Functions should be independent 44
Classes and structures 45
  Class fields (constants and variables) 46
Functions 47
  One thing 47
  Clueless 47
  Private 47
  Close by 47
  Do not use self 47
  Define them in the right place 48
  Extension 48
  Remove the useless functions 48
  Reduce the cyclomatic complexity 48
Closures 52
Control flow statements 52
Boolean values 53
Protocol Conformance 53
Ternary 53
Global parameters 54
Optionals 54
Beautify your code 55

Refactoring 57
Definition 57
When to refactor 57
When not to refactor 58
Bad smells in the code 59
How to refactor 61

Refactoring Methods 63
Extract method 63
Inline method 65
Move method 66
Introduce new method 68
Extract utility method 69
Extract surrounding method 71

Extract template method 73

Hide method 75

Introduce named parameter 76

Parameterize method 78

Preserve the whole object 79

Remove the named parameter 80

Remove the parameter 82

Rename method 83

Replace parameter with method 84

Replace method with method object 85

Encapsulate downcast 87

Refactoring Class fields 90

Move field 90

Eagerly initialized attribute 91

Pull up field 92

Hide field 93

Lazy initialized attribute 94

Refactoring Classes 96

Extract Class 96

Inline Class 98

Replace Array with an Object.......................................99

Change unidirectional association to bidirectional 100

Change bidirectional association to unidirectional 103

Collapse hierarchy..104

Replace Type Code with Polymorphism......................105

Extract protocol..108

Extract subclass..110

Extract superclass 111

Introduce Null object 113

Pull up constructor body 115

Pull up method..117

Push down field or method 118

Replace subclass with fields 119

Refactoring Variables..122

Introduce explaining variable.....................................122

Split temporary variable 123

Inline temp 123

Introduce Assertion...124

Refactoring Conditional 128

Consolidate conditional expressions 128
Consolidate Duplicate Conditional Fragments 129
Decompose conditional...130
Remove control flag...131
Simplify nested conditionals with returns 134

Refactoring Code..137
Replace type code with enumeration 137
Replace magic number with symbolic constants 138
Substitute algorithm...140

To be continued 143

Bibliography...145

Introduction

Scenario One

You are starting a new project using Swift or any other language.

You know the language pretty well.

You have all the requirements so you proceed to coding and deliver the project in time. All is good.

Scenario Two

Now imagine you have to work on a project together in a team of few developers. Each of them smart, but with different backgrounds: some experienced Swift programmers; some have just learned Swift as their first language. Some are experienced with Objective-C and switched to Swift. Some worked for a long time in Java and it is their first-time programming Swift so they are still going through the tutorials.

How do you do it? What kind of information do you provide them? How do you bring them in sync so the result is a product that works well, that is delivered in time, but that can also be built upon?

This book is the answer to that question. It contains the information you need to provide the team in order to have a smooth development process.

The book does not teach Swift. Also, it is not really about Swift. It contains the knowledge a developer needs after he or she learned the secrets of the programming language.

The book's aim is to help you write elegant code.

We like elegant people. We like stylish people. Elegant clothes are not always the most expensive though. Stylish clothes might cost a bit more but throwing money on clothes does not guarantee the success.

What about code, how can we define the elegant one?

Elegant code must be

- simple (so that anybody can understand it anytime in the future)
- short (as short as possible but not shorter than that)
- clear (does not use any ambiguous statements)
- easy to change
- performant (the code should be pretty fast and use only the resources it really needs)
- smart

Read on to learn few tricks for upgrading your code from working code to Code In Style.

Code standards

Code standards are similar to code manners. You can survive without it, but it would not be that fun.

Code manners are different from country to country. And that is okay. Just like it is okay for different teams to have different code standards. But having different code standards in the same team or worse, having no code standards at all is the recipe for ugly code, long maintenance time and unhappy developers.

This chapter is an example of a coding standards document. Feel free to change it in any way you and your team wants. As the whole team will use this, it needs to be discussed and changed and accepted by all.

Indenting

Indenting is important for code visibility and beauty. Compare this:

```
var value: Int = 9 {
    didSet {
        if (value < 1) || (value > 9) {
            print("DigitView: invalid value: \(value)")
            self.label.text = "?"
        } else {
            self.label.text = String(value)
        }
    }
}
```

with this

```
var value: Int = 9 { didSet { if (value < 1) || (value > 9) {
print("DigitView: invalid value: \(value)")
self.label.text = "?"
} else { self.label.text = String(value) } }
```

The second version was the result of trying to reduce the number of lines. I bet you did not even notice that one curly bracket is missing.

The default indenting for Xcode is four spaces and tabs will be converted to spaces. You can change this in Xcode preferences.

Line length

In the past, the rule was that the code should not exceed the screen. This was when the screen was 80 characters or so. With the huge resolution offered by retina display screens, now you can easily fit 200 or even 300 characters on a screen so the rule does not apply anymore.

Xcode recommends 120 characters on a line and it is also displaying a guideline. This limit should be good enough.

Sometimes, the lines really need to be longer than that, for example when having an array initialized in the code. In this case, place each item or bunch of them on separate lines.

For example, instead of:

```
let monthNames = ["January", "February", "March", "April",
"May", "June", "July", "August", "September", "October",
"November", "December"]
```

Use
```
 let monthNames = [
            "January",
            "February",
            "March",
            "April",
            "May",
            "June",
            "July",
            "August",
            "September",
            "October",
            "November",
            "December"]
```

or

```
let monthNames = [
           "January", "February", "March", "April",
           "May", "June", "July", "August",
           "September", "October", "November", "December"]
```

Semicolon

Even if Swift allows separating multiple function calls by semicolon, do not use this option.

Allow each function call on a separate line.

One of the beauties of Swift consists in getting rid of the useless semicolon.

Brackets

Round brackets

When combining more calculated Boolean values, use round brackets around each of them.

For example, even if the following is correct

```
if age > 18 && income > 50000 && city == "toronto" {
...
}
```

the following has a greater clarity

```
if (age > 18) && (income > 50000) && (city == "toronto") {
...
}
```

Curly brackets ("{" and "}")

An open curly bracket ("{") should sit on the same line as the function or the control flow statement (for, while, repeat, if, switch) preceding it. The closing one ("}") should have its own separate line.

```
let ageAsString = ""
if age < 10 {
    ageAsString = "0\(age)"
} else {
    ageAsString = "\(age)"
}
```

Empty spaces

Spaces increase code readability if used consistently.

Other than for indenting, there should not be more than one space around any coding entity. At the same time, lots of entities look better with a space around them.

Here are some examples:

Equal

Add a space at both ends of equal sign.
```
let x = 10
```

Arrays

Arrays should have no space after "[" and before "]".

```
let firstThreeMonthNames = ["January", "February", "March"]
```

Function

Add no spaces after a variable but one space before type.

Use no space after the function name and "(" but one space between ")" and "{"

```
override func viewDidAppear(animated: Bool) {
```

Variable declaration

Use not space after the variable name but one space before the type.

```
var age: Int
```

Boolean conditions

No space after "(" and before ")" but one space before "(" and one after ")".

```
if (age > 18) && (country == "Canada") {
    print ("Canadian adult")
}
```

Comparison

When using calculated Boolean values using "==", "<", ">", etc., add space on both sides.

```
if age == 18 {
    ...
}
```

as opposed to

```
if age==18 {
    ...
}
```

Comma

Use no space before and one space after comma.

```
let primeNumbers = [2, 3, 5, 7]
let firstThreeMonthNames = ["January", "February", "March"]
```

This is visually pleasing as it is a rule for writing a regular document, but also allows the line to be wrapped in case you resize the screen.

Empty lines

Add one empty line between entities (like functions or classes) or to separate some islands of code somehow related.

Adding more than one line is not useful.

See an example as follows.

```
//
//   Utils.swift
//   FluffyFly
//
//   Created by Dragos Ionel on 2015-04-30.
//   Copyright (c) 2015 Adelante Consulting Inc.
//   All rights reserved.

import UIKit
import Darwin
import AVFoundation

class Utils {

    class func setupAudioPlayerWithFile(file:NSString,
                    type:NSString) -> AVAudioPlayer  {

        var path = NSBundle.mainBundle().pathForResource(
            file as String, ofType: type as String)
        var url = NSURL.fileURLWithPath(path!)
        var error: NSError?

        var audioPlayer:AVAudioPlayer?
        audioPlayer = AVAudioPlayer(contentsOfURL: url,
            error: &error)
        if error != nil {
            NSLog("%@", error!.localizedDescription)
        }
        audioPlayer?.numberOfLoops = -1 //continuous play

        return audioPlayer!
    }
```

There is an empty line after the initial comment of the class.

We have one line after the import section and one line after the class name.

I also added one space between the first three variables and the rest of the code as it is dealing with initializing and configuring the audio player.

I also added a line between each of the previous paragraphs to prove the point. :-)

Naming

Introduction

Some time ago, I travelled to India and one of things that amazed me was that, after I was introducing myself, everybody was asking: "What does your name mean?"

"What do you mean what does it mean? It is a name, names mean nothing", I was thinking.

Of course, I was wrong. Most of the names mean something:

John means gracious.
Mary means sea.
Will means of course will, desire.
And so forth.

Even my name Dragos, comes from "drag" which means loved, in Romanian. My Indian friends were amazed when I was telling them that. I guess they were seeing the contradiction of the name and the reality. Luckily, they did not think to the meaning of 'drag' in English...

How about the entities we use in our code?

Why is a name important?

The name might not seem important as you are writing the code. You know the name, you know what the particular variable or constant is for and all is great. But if the code is read by somebody else or even by you after a while, the knowledge you have now will not be available. All that will be available will be the variable name and the context. And the context is not that much there as the developer reading your code might just look at a piece of the code only and not at the whole class. A piece of code spends far more time under maintenance phase than development phase.

Imagine a piece of code like the following:

```
if x < 10 {
    x = x + 1
}
```

There is little chance its purpose can be understood just by looking at it.

Variables and constants

One friend told me that while he was reviewing some code, he noticed that all the variables had cryptic names: aaa, AbC, temp, xx, Y, etc. When he asked the author why he used such strange names, the guy replied: "Because it does not even matter, the compiler is changing the names anyway."

That would be okay if nobody is ever changing the code. But we know that is never the case.

Here are few rules about naming a variable or a constant:

Choose a rule for capitalizing and stick to it

In Swift, lower camel case is mostly used. For constants, start the name with a "k".

```
var age:Int
var userAddress:String
let kMinutesPerHour = 60
```

Names are nouns

For example:

```
var carName: String
var distance, timeInMinutes: Int
```

but no:

```
var compute, decide: Int
```

Exception, the Boolean values that can be past participle:

```
var found, crashed: Bool
```

Who are you?

The name must answer to the question:

"Who are you?"

"I am [variable name]"

For example:

"I am `homeViewController`" sounds good.

"I am `storesViewController`" sounds not.

No comment needed

The name should be carefully chosen that it does not require a comment explaining its purpose. If it does, it is not a good name.

For example, replace:

```
var time: Int //in seconds
```

with

```
var timeInSeconds: Int
```

Add a comment only when you want to add more information about the variable.

```
//used to decide if the system should enter sleep mode
var timeInSeconds: Int
```

Often, we need to go through multiple iterations before a good name is chosen. If no name seems good enough, choose whatever, add a comment (//FIXME: change the name), and revisit it later. For sure, in time, a better name will be found.

Speak English

Use English words and make the names readable.

If somebody calls you on the phone and asks you about the name of the variable, you should have no issue saying it without the need to spell it.

userName is good but bnkVldUser is not a good one even if you know it is a bank valued customer.

Be specific

When choosing a name try to be as specific as possible.

For example:

userName is good.

name is not. Whose name? User's name, first name, last name, dog's name?

user is a good name only if it means a user object. But if it means the user name or user id, it is not a good choice.

Context

Consider the variables and the constants as thieves that steal memory, processor cycles and developer attention. Hide them as much as you can in the most restrictive context possible.

If the variable is used only in a function, make it local to the function. If only a class uses it, make it private.

If you are not sure if a variable needs to be private, make it so and you will find out.

It is rare when you need global variables.

If you need global constants, add them in the class where it makes the most sense. If it doesn't, create a separate file for constants.

Shortest but no shorter than that

Make the variable name as short as possible, but no shorter than that. Also make it as long as needed.

Swift is following the tradition of Objective-C that is known for long names.

If you need to name a variable `userNameBeforeEnteringLoginScreen` so be it. With the modern IDE, one rarely needs to type a full name as the tool is autocompleting it for you.

When using long names, try not to make them too similar, as they can be confused one to another.

For example, `userNameBeforeEnteringLoginScreen` and `userNameBeforeEnteringLogoutScreen` are not good choices.

Never use negations in Boolean values

Try to understand the following code quickly:

```
var isNotLogged, isNotAdmin: Bool
...
if !(!isNotLogged && !isNotAdmin) {
    print("Huh?!?")
}
```

Replacing the previous code with the following makes more sense

```
var isLogged, isAdmin: Bool
...
if !(isLogged && isAdmin) {
    print("It is not logged in nor it is an admin")
}
```

Unit of measure

Adding the unit of measure is sometime useful for clarifying the purpose of a variable.

Here is an example:

```
class Movie {
    func length () -> Int {
        return 1000
    }
}
```

What is the unit for length? Seconds, minutes, hours?

A better name would be `lengthInSeconds`.

Add the types at the end of variable name

The Hungarian notation, used by Microsoft when developing Microsoft Windows, added the type name at the beginning of each variable name:

`iAge` - age as an Integer
`sName` - name as a string

`arrUsers` - an array of users

We are not recommending this, as Swift is a strong type language so the chance of issues caused by not remembering the variable type is slim.

Nevertheless, in the case of certain types it is useful to include part of the object type at the end of the variable.

For example:

```
let loginButton = UIButton()
let loginView = UIView()
let homeViewController = UIViewController()
let userArray = NSMutableArray()
```

This will allow the following code to need no explanation:

```
loginView.addSubview(loginButton)
homeViewController.view.addSubview(loginView)
```

Don't be creative

Do not invent your own convention. For example, do not consider adding `str` for each string or `nbr` for each number when nobody does that.

Adding a document with the convention might not help as there is a big chance nobody will read it and let alone update it.

Regarding documentation, write your code assuming nobody will read any documentation you used to create the code nor any other documentation you produce to explain the code.

Do not be smarty pants

While a name might look funny to you, it might not for others. You might confuse the next developer.

For example: `dyingWish` for a crash message ain't a good name.

Nor is

```
var tro: Bool
```

It is a bit funny though.

Functions

Whatcha doin'?

While the variables are the nouns of the coding (as we've seen), the functions are the verbs.

To be sure they have a correct name, ask them:

"Whatcha doin'?"

"I [function name]" should be the answer.

"I `createDatabase`" - is good.

"I `sortArray`" - is great.

"I `user`" - not that much.

"I `database`" - nop.

Also, the order of the words is important. First one should be a verb:

"I `createDatabase`" is good.

"I `databaseCreate`" is okay, but only if your name is Yoda.

Capitalization

A function name should use lower camel case. It should start with an imperative verb.

```
func getUserName() {
    ...
}
```

Be specific

The name should be explicit:

`create` is a good name, but not clear. Create what: a variable, a database, a singleton?

Long is okay

The same as for variables make the name of the function as long as you need, but not longer than that.

For example, `createLocalDatabase` might be replaced with `createDatabase` if there is only one database.

Function name should describe clearly what it does. The parameters should follow variables naming standards, clearly describing their purpose.

Do not save space when naming a function. If making the name longer adds clarity, so be it.

Check the name of this function from UIViewController:

```
public func transitionFromViewController(
      fromViewController: UIViewController,
      toViewController: UIViewController,
      duration: NSTimeInterval,
      options: UIViewAnimationOptions,
      animations: (() -> Void)?,
```

```
completion: ((Bool) -> Void)?)
```

Function parameters

- Hunny!
- Yes, hunny!
- Can you please run to the store and get few things?
- For sure, hunny! What do you need?
- I need bread, eggs, cheese, milk, apples and pears. Get 2, a dozen, a pound, 2 liters, a bag and 4 or 5!

*

Funny eh? This is how some languages define the functions. Luckily, Objective-C and Swift are different. You can use named parameters that make the life easier.

The rules for naming a function parameter are similar with those for variables:

- the name should make it clear what is its purpose

- it can be as long as needed, but not longer than that

- use lower camel case capitalization rule

Number of parameters

The parameters should be as few as possible.

Uncle Bob (aka Robert C. Martin) says in his "Clean Code" book:

"The ideal number of arguments for a function is zero (niladic). Next comes one (monadic), followed closely by two (dyadic). Three arguments (triadic) should be avoided where possible. More than three (polyadic) requires very special justification—and then shouldn't be used anyway."

If you do require more than three parameters, then it might be the time to refactor and pack those parameters into their own class.

Classes and structures

Classes and structures are the building block of the code. They are used to pack together properties and functions. Naming them is of great importance.

Use nouns for their names.

Classes usually have the same name, as the file they are in so using only letters is advisable.

As classes and structures are very similar in purpose and use, so we'll look at them together.

Capitalization

Classes and structures names should use upper camel case.

For example: `HomeViewController`.

Be specific

A name of a class should be chosen in such a way that it clearly describes what it does. If a comment is needed to explain what the class does, then the name is not good enough.

This is even more important than variable name. A variable is most probably used in the same file as it is defined, but a class will be used across the project and navigating to the file that defined the class each time to find out what it does is used is a waste of time.

As long as it need

Feel free to use longer names.

No prefix

There is no need to prefix the class with a certain set of letters to describe the project. Swift classes are automatically name spaced by the module that contains them. If two names from different modules collide you can disambiguate by prefixing the type name with the module name.

```
let myClass = MyModule.UsefulClass()
```

Types

The name of a type should be an upper camel case compound word made of nouns (mostly).

```
typealias UserNameType = String
```

Enumerations

Use camel case for enumeration values:

```
enum Shape {
  case rectangle
  case square
  case triangle
  case circle
}
```

Projects

For projects, use short and simple names, making clear what the project is about. This name is used in creating folders so preferably don't use any space or non-letter characters. If you have multiple words, use camel case with starting capital.

For example: `SimpleSudoku`

The project name is also used for creating the bundle name and if it is simple enough, it will be used as is. For example:

```
ca.adelante.SimpleSudoku
```

If you use two words (for example `Simple Sudoku`), Xcode will change the name to have a valid identifier (`ca.adelante.Simple-Sudoku`).

Libraries

A library in Xcode is a special kind of a project, but a project nevertheless. Use the same rules as above.

Name needs to be chosen in such a way, that it is clear what the library does. For example, `NetworkServices`, for a library that deals with network, or `QRCodeUtility` for a library that deals with QR Codes.

While `SimpleSudoku` is just fine for the name of a Sudoku game, for a library it would just confuse people. Is it a library that is generating a Sudoku? It is solving one? Or it is just a database of games? And why "simple"? It is just for simple games?

General notes about naming

Avoid ambiguous names

For example, the following names can be confusing:

```
User.getName
Location.getDistance
City.getTime
```

Better names are:

```
User.getFirstName
```

```
User.getFullName
Location.getDistanceFromCurrentPositionInMiles
City.getTimeInUT
```

How long is too long

In Objective-C as well as in Swift the length of the variables is not really an issue.

See some examples from class UIViewController:

```
transitionFromViewController
(_:toViewController:duration:options:animations: completion:)
modalPresentationCapturesStatusBarAppearance
UIViewControllerShowDetailTargetDidChangeNotification
```

So, feel free to usc longer names if it makes sense.

As most of the modern code editors, Xcode has code completion so you will probably never need to type the whole function of variable name.

Also use shorter names if the scope of a variable is shorter.

For example, i is a default name for an iterator variable.

```
var i:Int
for i in 1...5 {
    print("square of \(i) is \(i*i)")
}
```

For a global variable though, the name should be longer describing its purpose.

Adding a comment for a name helps only a little as the entity will be used most of the time in other places then where it is defined.

Remove useless words

Remove the words that are not needed from the names.

For example, the bold words do not bring any more clarity to the following functions:

```
class User {
    func get**User**Name(){
    }
}

class Database {
    func init**LocalDatabase**(){
    }
}

class Game {
    func restart**Game**() {
    }

    func invite**Another**User() {
    }
}
```

Worst enemy: misleading names

A misleading name is worse than a bad name.

Imagine a class `User` with a property with two properties: `address` and `homeAddress`. While `homeAddress` is clear, what is `address`?

If this property is used in a different object as:

```
user.address = "..."
```

Any developer might wrongly guess that this is the home address.

Comments

Introduction

"Documentation is the code" some say.

"Add as much comments as possible, they will be useful" others say.

"My code is obvious, it does not need comments", we, all the developers, think.

When it comes to commenting the code, there is no doubt that it is a useful activity. But when it comes to doing it, we are happy not to do it. It is something that brings no benefit in the short run. It is just consuming time and as the time is always short we like to skip it or postpone it for later, which actually means the same thing. "I'll add comments later" is something that never happens.

When to use comments

Comments in the code should be used only when naming fails to explain thoroughly the code.

If a comment is needed, the first option should be to try to improve the code so it does not need an explanation. As we've seen in the Naming chapter, variables, constants, functions, and classes names should be chosen with so much care that any developer, with little or no knowledge of our code, should be able to understand it without digging too much.

Document "Why"

This is the information you can include in the comments:

1. WHY the code does what it does. Why the code is written.

2. WHAT it does, but this only if it is really necessary.

3. HOW it does is the last thing, as priority, you should document. This should be pretty straightforward from the code. If not, the code needs to be refactored.

Of course, there are exceptions. If the code uses an algorithm that is not common knowledge (for example, calculating a pair of public - private keys), then it might be useful to document how the code is achieving the result.

Only if needed

There is no point in commenting a code that is obvious.

For example, the following comments are useless:

```
//age of the user
let userAge: Int

//increment the index
index += 1
```

Do not use a comment to "translate" the code in English. Swift allows you to write the code in such a way that is very close to English.

```
func drawACircleAtPoint(point:Point, radius:Double){
    ...
}
```

When calling the function as follows

```
drawACircleAtPoint(screenCenterPoint, radius:10)
```

a comment like

```
//draw a circle at screenCenterPoint with radius 10
```

would be useless.

Comments are not code

If the code is not clear, do not comment to improve it. Fix the code as much as possible. Do not use comments to improve bad code.

The comments should be replaced by code as much as possible.

Mark code

While you should not use the comments to improve your bad code, there are cases when you want to mark a certain code in a certain way.

For example:

```
//TODO: this works but it needs to be refactored
//as it duplicates the code in Utils class
```

Of course, in a perfect world the developer should refactor it on the spot. But, sometimes there are reasons he cannot do it:
- the issue he is working on is not related to the bad piece of code
- he does not have the knowledge to fix it
- it will take a long time to fix it
- there is a big risk in doing it
- the current task is urgent, for example a critical production issue, and business reasons are stronger than refactoring and code beauty

Here is a list of the tags you can use for this in comments:

MARK:

Use MARK: to separate code with similar functionality. It is the equivalent to #pragma mark from Objective-C and allows the developer to jump easily from one section to another.

For example:

```
// MARK: digit management
func setDigitAt(x x:Int, y:Int, value:Int) {
    self.digitArray[x][y] = value
}

func getDigitAt(x x:Int, y:Int) -> Int {
    return digitArray[x][y]
}
```

Will be displayed by Xcode:

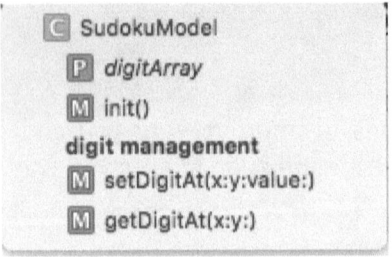

The space between "//" and "MARK" is ignored but semicolon should follow "MARK".

Adding a "-" after the semicolon will add a line of separation between sections:

```
// MARK:- digit management
```

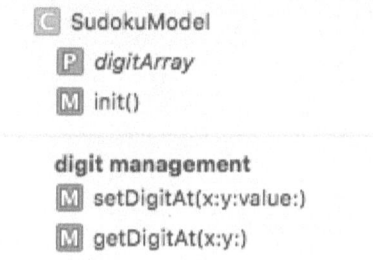

TODO:

Use it for marking an area of code that needs to be completed. This can be used during development and, theoretically, should not be present when the code is shared with others. The code in the repository should always have the features completed and fully tested.

For example:

```
// TODO: make the init private
init() {
}
```

This will result in:

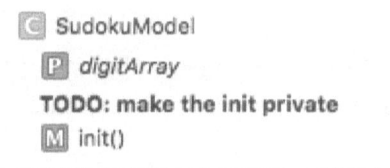

FIXME:

This should have even a shorter life than TODO. It marks an area of code that is not working properly and should be fixed as soon as possible.

```
//FIXME: the function is not returning the correct result
func calculateComplexity() -> Int {
    return digitArray.count
}
```

will result in:

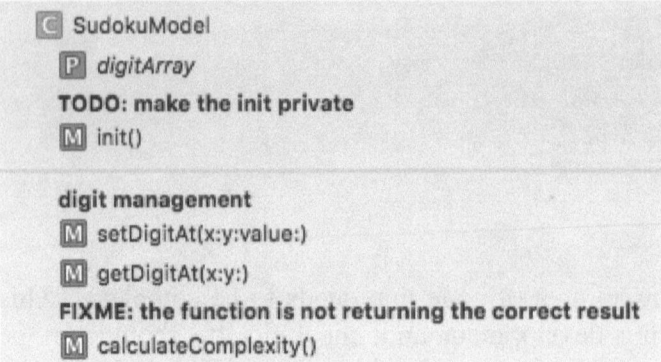

Document your thoughts

Use comments to record your thought process. Sometimes you have to go through many iterations until you implement certain functionality. You might use some documentation, some online resources or research. These are not available to the next developer looking at your code so he or she might not get it. Couple of lines of comments can go a long way.

Imagine you are walking a colleague through your code. What are the things you would tell him or her? Those are the things you should add into the comments.

Libraries

For libraries, extra care and effort should be shown as they are used by developers who know nothing of their code, nor do they have access to it. Also, they might be using just one piece of code, like a function, without any knowledge of the rest of the library.

Do not comment junk

Do not keep the code for the future, by commenting it. One can see the history in the code versioning control system.

So, code like this should not exist in a repository:

```
//    func getDigitAt(x x:Int, y:Int) -> Int {
//        return digitArray[x][y]
//    }
```

Of course, this is okay during code development and refactoring. You might think a function is not used so commenting it for a time being might allow to you revert it in case the code starts crashing. But when you are ready to commit to repository, all this code should be deleted.

Xcode makes it easy to see all the changes by launching Source Control -> Commit.

There you can see all the changes and also edit the ones you don't need. After making any changes, you should cancel the commit and run your code. You know, just in case you screwed up something.

Comment bigger chunks of code.

When you add a comment make it for a bigger section of your code as opposed to commenting each line. Make it like a story: "this code is for this…" then some code, then "this code is for this". In this way, a developer can follow the story of your code even if he does not fully understand how the code is working.

Keep it short

Keep comments precise and compact. And also in English.

Make it clear and up to date

The comment should be crystal clear about your intention. Also bring the comments up to date if the code they are referring to us updated. Worse than having no comments at all is having wrong comments in the code.

Don't be funny.

Avoid something like:

```
//destroy the universe
reset = true
```

Or:

```
// Dear maintainer:
//
// Once you are done trying to 'optimize' this routine,
// and have realized what a terrible mistake that was,
// please increment the following counter as a warning
// to the next guy:
//
// total_hours_wasted_here = 42
```

(source: http://stackoverflow.com)

Actually, this was funny!

Don't be an artist

You are allowed to be an artist, but not in the comments section.

```
/*
  (c).-.(c)      (c).-.(c)      (c).-.(c)      (c).-.(c)      (c).-.(c)      (c).-.(c)
  / ._. \        / ._. \        / ._. \        / ._. \        / ._. \        / ._. \
 __\( Y )/__    __\( Y )/__    __\( Y )/__    __\( Y )/__    __\( Y )/__    __\( Y )/__
(_.-/'-'\-._)  (_.-/'-'\-._)  (_.-/'-'\-._)  (_.-/'-'\-._)  (_.-/'-'\-._)  (_.-/'-'\-._)
   || M ||         || O ||         || N ||         || K ||         || E ||         || Y ||
  _.' `-' '._     _.' `-' '._     _.' `-' '._     _.' `-' '._     _.' `-' '._     _.' `-' '._
 (.-./`-'\.-.)   (.-./`-'\.-.)   (.-./`-'\.-.)   (.-./`-'\.-.)   (.-./`-'\.-.)   (.-./`-'\.-.)
  `-'     `-'      `-'     `-'     `-'     `-'     `-'     `-'     `-'     `-'     `-'     `-'

              -It's Monkey Business Time! (Version 1.5)
*/
```

(Source http://improvingsoftware.com/)

Don't track the history

Do not document the history in the comments area. That is what source control is for.

```
/*
Class created by John Doe on 2015/01/03
Changed but Jimmy to add a new function on 2015/03/02
Refactored by John to remove the function Jimmy added as it is
useless on 2015/04/01
Changed by Jimmy to add back the function John removed on
2015/05/04
*/
```

This kind of comments can grow exponentially and provide no benefit at all.

Commits

When the code is committed to a source control system, a comment needs to be provided. Some systems make it mandatory.

This comment has multiple purposes:
- make it clear what the change was about
- allows in the future to look at the history in case the issue is found again
- allows to inspect the code at each line level to see who changed the code by using Blame option
- allows to inspect the code to see why it was added

In case you never used it, Blame option is accessed by long clicking "Show the Version Editor":

It allows you to find who wrote each line of code, in other words find somebody to blame for bad code. Lots of times, that person is actually you.

Syntax

Single line comments start with // . It is supposed to be used for short comments

Multiple line comments starting with /* and ending with */

Swift allows the comments to be embedded, so the following is a valid code:

```
/*
//this is a comment
/*
this is another
*/

let kSize = 9
*/
```

Markup

The aim of the comment markup is twofold:

It allows tools like Headerdoc to export nice documentation from your code.

Empower you or any other developer to get more information about the code,

In the following, we'll look more into point two.

How to visualize markup in Xcode

Assume we have the following code with markup:

```
///alpha for selected digit
let kAlphaSelected = 0.7
```

There are three ways of visualizing the markup for a symbol.

The first way is in the Quick Help Inspector.

Move the cursor on the symbol you want to inspect and open Quick Inspector (View -> Utilities -> Show Quick Help Inspector)

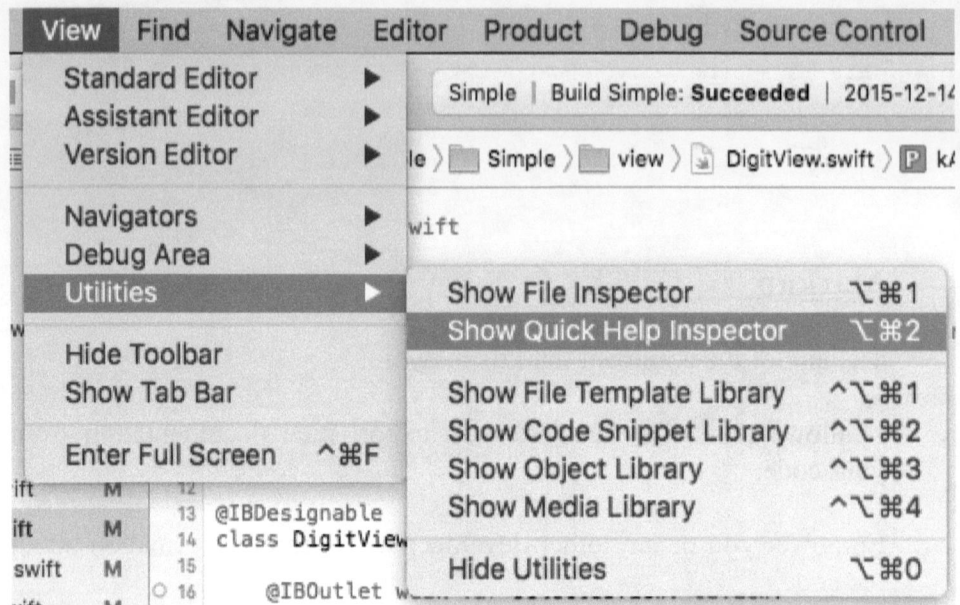

The result is something like this:

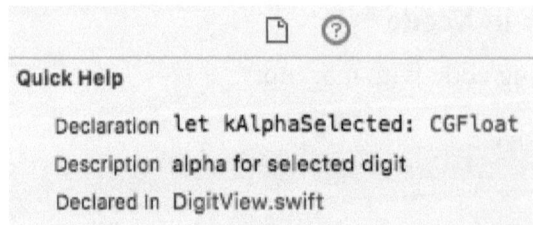

The second option is to Option + Click the symbol. The result:

```
ests                     21        ///alpha for selected digit
                         22        let kAlphaSelected: CGFloat = 0.7
cuMo ITest.swift M       23
ig        Declaration  let kAlphaSelected: CGFloat
a:
e]        Description  alpha for selected digit
          Declared In  DigitView.swift
ITests                   29        super.loadViewFromNib(kNibFileName)
```

Also, Xcode displays automatically the description to the symbol completion while you type:

```
}
                 alpha for selected digit
@IBAct
    DL   V   CGFloat kAlphaSelected
    sender.alpha = kAlphaSelected
}
```

Where to add markup code

You can add markup code before any symbol you want to add more details about: constant, variable, function, class, type.

If the code will be made available or it is part of a bigger application where you and other developers have full access, then you should follow the rules from previous paragraphs. Document only what makes sense. If a comment is useless, it will stay useless even if beautifully markuped (I know there is not such a word as markuped, but it should be invented).

If you are working on a library, then you need to document all the public symbols as their users will not have access to the code.

Markup code syntax

Markup code is a comment so it has a similar structure.

Single line markup

For single line comment, use "///" at the beginning of each line. For example:

```
///called when a cell in the board is tapped
///for now just adjust the alpha

@IBAction func tapRecognized(sender: UIButton) {
    DLog("tap recognized")
    sender.alpha = kAlphaSelected
}
```

Will result in:

```
Quick Help
    Declaration  @IBAction func tapRecognized(sender:
                 UIButton)
    Description  called when a cell in the board is tapped for
                 now just adjust the alpha
    Declared In  DigitView.swift
```

There can be multiple lines starting with "///".

All the lines are concatenated with a space in between. If you wish to start a new line, add an empty line.

The empty lines between the last line starting with "///" and the symbol are ignored.

There cannot be any other items except empty lines in between, otherwise the markup will not be attached to this symbol.

Block markup

The block markup has the following syntax:

```
/**
text
*/
```

For example:
```
/**
called when a cell in the board is tapped

for now just adjust the alpha
*/
@IBAction func tapRecognized(sender: UIButton) {
    DLog("tap recognized")
    sender.alpha = kAlphaSelected
}
```

Will result in:

Declaration `@IBAction func tapRecognized(sender: UIButton)`

Description called when a cell in the board is tapped

for now just adjust the alpha

Declared In DigitView.swift

The same as for single line comments, all the lines are concatenated except for empty lines.

Special commands

Other than regular text, you can enter special commands that have a different meaning and are processed different by Xcode. For each of them the format is:

```
- command text: text
```

Parameter

Use this to add information about a parameter. Use it for when the function has only one parameter.

```
/**
Called when a cell in the board is tapped
- parameter sender: The button that triggered this function
*/
@IBAction func tapRecognized(sender: UIButton) {
     DLog("tap recognized")
     sender.alpha = kAlphaSelected
}
```

results in:

Declaration `@IBAction func tapRecognized(sender: UIButton)`

Description Called when a cell in the board is tapped

Parameters sender

The button that triggered this function

Declared In DigitView.swift

Parameters

Use it when the function has multiple parameters. It is equivalent to adding multiple parameters sections.

```
/**
 Returns the maximum of two values
 - parameters:
   - firstValue: the first value to be compared
   - secondValue: the second value to be compared
 */
func max(firstValue firstValue:Int, secondValue:Int) -> Int {
    if firstValue > secondValue {
        return firstValue
    }
    return secondValue
}
```

will result in

Quick Help

Declaration	`func max(firstValue firstValue: Int, secondValue: Int) -> Int`
Description	Returns the maximum of two values
Parameters	`firstValue`
	the first value to be compared
	`secondValue`
	the second value to be compared
Declared In	Utils.swift

Returns

Used to specify the value returned by a function.

The following code:

```
/**
 - returns: maximum of two values
 */
func max(firstValue firstValue:Int, secondValue:Int) -> Int {
```

```
    if firstValue > secondValue {
        return firstValue
    }
    return secondValue
}
```

will result in:

Quick Help

   Declaration `func max(firstValue firstValue: Int, secondValue: Int) -> Int`

     Returns maximum of two values

   Declared In main.swift

Throws

Used to specify the error that can be thrown.

```
/**
 - throws: for now, nothing
 */
func max(firstValue firstValue:Int, secondValue:Int) -> Int {
    if firstValue > secondValue {
        return firstValue
    }
    return secondValue
}
```

will result in

Quick Help

   Declaration `func max(firstValue firstValue: Int, secondValue: Int) -> Int`

     Throws for now, nothing

   Declared In Utils.swift

Coding with grace

Introduction

In Swift as well as in any other programming languages, you can achieve the same result in two or more ways. Choosing one of them is a matter of preference or a matter of how others are doing it. We'll go through different such cases and we'll suggest one way of doing it. Feel free to accept the solution or to adopt any other one if you have a reason for it.

This chapter is mostly about Swift. If you are using a different programming language, feel free to go quickly through it or skip it altogether.

Variables and constants

Types

For variables and constants that are initialized when they are defined, Swift allows the type to be inferred. You have the option to specify the type as well, to increase clarity or for cases when the type you desire is different than the one inferred.

For example:

```
var ageLimitInYears: Int = 18
```

is equivalent to

```
var ageLimitInYears = 18
```

We suggest you use the last form.

There are cases when the type inference is not what you want. The age limit, in the above case, might be a float number, so the correct code would be:

```
var ageLimitInYears: Float = 18
```

Location for constants

If one constant is used across multiple files, define them in the class where it makes most sense.

If there are multiple constants used across different classes and there is not clear where it should be defined, use a separate file for all the constants.

Functions should be independent

Do not use class variables to pass information among class functions.

They should be as independent as possible.

For example, consider the following class:

```
class Address {
    var street = "", city = "", country = ""
    private var fullAddress=""

    func generateFullAddress() {
        self.fullAddress = "\(self.street), \(self.city),
            \(self.country)"
    }

    func getFormattedAddress() -> String {
        return "Your address is \(self.fullAddress)"
    }
}
```

```
var address = Address()
address.street = "9 Lemmon St."
address.city = "Toronto"
address.country = "Canada"

print(address.getFormattedAddress())
```

The code will print nothing, of course. We forgot to call generateCompactAddress to populate the full address.

A better solution is:

```
class Address {
    var street = "", city = "", country = ""

    func generateCompactAddress() -> String {
        return "\(self.street), \(self.city), \(self.country)"
    }

    func getFormattedAddress() -> String {
        return "Your address is \(generateCompactAddress())"
    }
}

var address = Address()
address.street = "9 Lemmon St."
address.city = "Toronto"
address.country = "Canada"

print(address.getFormattedAddress())
```

The code will now work correctly and we got rid of a variable.

Classes and structures

Classes and structures need to do one thing and do it well. Also, as much as possible, should hide their internal functionality from other classes.

They should contain the minimum number of components (variables, constants, functions).

Class fields (constants and variables)

Private

A field should be private, unless it is needed otherwise. Skip the default modifiers (like internal).

Constants

Make everything a constant (using let) unless it needs to be a variable.

Give it space

Each field should be defined on a separate line, unless it shares a common purpose with other ones.

Do not define multiple variables on the same line just because they are the same type.

For example, instead of

```
var age, passwordLength: Int
```
use

```
var age: Int
var passwordLength: Int
```

On a separate topic, while `passwordLength` is clearly in characters, `age` is a bit confusing: what is the age in? Days, years, centuries?

A better version can be:

```
var ageInYears: Int
```

Use self

When using instance variables, use self to differentiate from local variables.

See below an example:

```
class User {
    var firstName, lastName: String

    func getFullName() -> String {
        return "\(self.firstName) \(self.lastName)"
    }
}
```

From this simple example, it might not be obvious the advantage, but keeping this rule might help us in other situations like the one following:

```
func update(firstName: String, lastName: String) {
    self.firstName = firstName
    self.lastName = lastName
}
```

Functions

One thing

A function should do just one thing.

Clueless

A function should use the data only from the parent class or from the parameters it receives.

Private

By default, a function should be private, unless otherwise needed.

Close by

The function should be declared as close as possible to the place where it is used. If multiple functions are called from different places, a special section with related functions can be created and labeled using MARK.

Do not use self

Even if allowed, do not use self when calling a local function as it is clear what function is called.

Define them in the right place

Add functions inside the classes only if it makes sense. Otherwise you can define them outside any class, as global function.

Extension

If a function works on a particular type (for example deciding if a string is a palindrome) consider extending that particular class to include the new functionality.

If you can extract a chunk of functionality as a separate function, please do so.

Remove the useless functions

Do not include any default implementation of functions.

```
override func viewDidLoad() {
    super.viewDidLoad()
}
```

Reduce the cyclomatic complexity

The cyclomatic complexity defines the number of possible paths a piece of code can follow. It can be a whole app or a function.

For example:

```
func printHello() {
    print("Hello")
}
```

There is only one option of execution, so the complexity is 1.

The following function has complexity 2, as there are two possible paths:

```
func checkIfTeenager(age:Int) {
    if age < 13 {
        print("not teenager")
    } else {
        print("teenager")
    }
}
```

While there is some debate about what complexity should be maximum, some say 3 some say 10, it is clear that the smaller it is the better.

Here are some suggestions to reduce it.

Example 1

```
func checkIfPositive(n:Int) -> Bool {
    if n > 0 {
        return true
    } else {
        return false
    }
}
```
The function has the complexity 2 as there are two different paths.

The more if-s one adds, the bigger the complexity is.

We can eliminate the if, and thus reducing the complexity, by returning directly the Boolean:

```
func checkIfPositive(n:Int) -> Bool {
    return (n > 0)
}
```

Example 2

```
func convertToString(n:Int) -> String {
    switch n {
    case 0:
        return "zero"
    case 1:
```

```
        return "one"
case 2:
        return "two"
case 3:
        return "three"
case 4:
        return "four"
case 5:
        return "five"
case 6:
        return "six"
case 7:
        return "seven"
case 8:
        return "eight"
case 9:
        return "nice"
default:
        return "unknown"
    }
}
```

This ugly function has complexity 11. It also has ugliness 1000, but that is not a measure that is invented yet.

What to do?

We can replace the ugly function with:

```
func convertToString(n:Int) -> String {
    if (n<0) || (n>9) {
        return "unknown"
    }

    let numberAsString = ["zero", "one", "two", "three",
        "four", "five", "six", "seven", "eight", "nine"]
    return numberAsString[n]
}
```

In this case, the complexity is down to 3.

Example 3

Here is another example. Consider a function that solves the second-degree equation:

```
///resolves a second-degree equation of the form a*x^2+b*x+c
func solveEquation(a: Float, b: Float, c: Float) -> String {

    if a == 0 {
        if b == 0 {
            if c == 0 {
                return("Any number is a solution")
            } else {
                return("there is no solution")
            }
        } else {
            let x = -c / b
            return "solution is \(x)"
        }
    } else {
        let delta = b*b - 4*a*c
        if delta < 0 {
            return "there is no solution"
        } else if delta == 0 {
            let x =   -b/(2*a)
            return "the solution is \(x)"
        } else {
            let x1 = (-b + sqrt(delta))/(2*a)
            let x2 = (-b + sqrt(delta))/(2*a)
            return  "the solutions are \(x1) and \(x2)"
        }
    }
}
```

The function has a complexity seven which is not bad, but we can reduce it by creating separate functions for separate sections of the code.

We notice that there are 3 general cases that the function is considering: when a, b or c are zero. We realize that the function is solving not only second-degree equation, but also first-degree equation and also the particular case when x does not appear in the equation. Let's call this zero degree equation.

We can extract each piece of code into a different function so that our code will look like this:

```
func solveEquation(a: Float, b: Float, c: Float) -> String {
    if a == 0 {
        return solveEquation1(b, c)
    } else {
        return solveEquation2(a, b, c)
    }
}

func solveEquation2(a: Float, b: Float, c: Float) -> String {
    let delta = b*b - 4*c*a
    if delta < 0 {
        return "there is no solution"
    } else if delta == 0 {
        let x = -b/(2*a)
        return "the solution is \(x)"
    } else {
        let x1 = (-b + sqrt(delta))/(2*a)
        let x2 = (-b + sqrt(delta))/(2*a)
        return "the solutions are \(x1) and \(x2)"
    }
}

func solveEquation1(b: Float, c: Float) -> String {
    if b == 0 {
        return solveEquation0(c)
    } else {
        let x = -c / b
        return "solution is \(x)"
    }
}

func solveEquation0(c: Float) -> String {
    if c == 0 {
        return "Any number is a solution"
    } else {
        return "there is no solution"
    }
}
```

We decreased the maximum complexity of the functions in our code from 7 to 3 (that is the complexity of `solveEquation2`).

Closures

When declaring an inline closure, avoid repeating parameter and return value types, because the compiler can always infer them.

If the closure is at the end, use the trailing closure syntax.

Control flow statements

Do not embed too many control flow statements (if, for, repeat, while, etc.) in too many levels. If you have more than 2 levels, you probably need to refactor or extract some code into a separate function.
See the refactoring methods for conditionals.

Boolean values

If the condition for the flow statements combines more than two - three calculated Boolean values, you probably need to define some constants for chunks of conditions.

See the refactoring methods for conditionals.

Protocol Conformance

Add a separate class extension for each protocol conformance. This greatly improves the code clarity and speeds up the changes

Preferred:

```
class MyViewcontroller: UIViewController {
  // class stuff here
}

extension MyViewcontroller: UITableViewDataSource {
  // table view data source methods
}

extension MyViewcontroller: UIScrollViewDelegate {
  // scroll view delegate methods
}
```

Not Preferred:

```
class MyViewcontroller: UIViewController,
            UITableViewDataSource, UIScrollViewDelegate {
}
```

Ternary

It is useful but it reduces the clarity of the code

First write if/else statement then change to ternary if it makes sense.

Let's revisit the example from solving the second-degree equation.

The following function:

```
func solveEquation0(c: Float) -> String {
    if c == 0 {
        return("Any number is a solution")
    } else {
        return("there is no solution")
    }
}
```

can also be written as:

```
func solveEquation01(c:Float) -> String {
    return (c == 0) ? "Any number is a solution" : "there is
no solution"
}
```

The second version provides less clarity and it does not fit on the screen either.

Global parameters

As much as possible do not use them. They are accessible to the whole name space and one doesn't know who is accessing and changing it.

If you need a global variable used across multiple classes, create a utility class that takes care of setting and retrieving it.

Otherwise there is the risk that a developer, confusing a local variable with a global one, will change the latter.

Optionals

When using optional bindings, use the same name as the variable you are unwrapping.

```
var age: Int?
if let age = age {
    …
}
```

If you age multiple unwrapping, put them on the same line

```
var price: Double?
var tax: Double?
var finalPrice: Double

if let price = price, let tax = tax {
    finalPrice = price * tax
}
```

Beautify your code

It might be funny to talk about beauty in coding, but maybe it is not.

We like to be surrounded by beautiful, whatever beautiful means for us.

We like a beautiful car, a beautiful house, a beautiful carpet. Of course, we like our spouse to be a beautiful woman or a handsome guy, on the case.

Nature is beautiful and so are most of the animals. The world is generally a beautiful place. The universe is beautiful and a starry night or a blue sky gives you great inner peace.

But why not the code? The long list of words and symbols that only geeks can understand can provide as much joy as a walk on the beach. Of course, only if you are a geek.

Beauty in the code has a very practical purpose: it increases the happiness of the developer. A happy developer writes better code increasing the productivity of the whole team and the performance of the product.

Making code beautiful and keeping it that way makes totally business sense.

Also, we might think that programming means writing code. But actually, writing the code is only a small percentage of the job (as a guess around 20%). All the other time is spent in reading others or our own code so how the code looks makes a big difference.

As beauty is a personal preference, so is beautiful code. So, decide what beautiful means to you, and build the code accordingly.

Refactoring

Definition

Refactoring is the activity of cleaning the code, improving the design, after the code is written.

Refactoring is not changing the functionality of the code. If it does, it is called maintenance.

You can say that it is corresponding to the design phase, but after some piece of code was written.

While a developer can plan for the code to be nicely written, in time, the code gets messier so cleaning is required.

Just like the house cleaning, the more often the code is cleaned, the easier and more effective it is.

Refactoring does not bring any benefit right away. The functionality is not changed so there is no change for the user. The real benefit is when new features are added or other developers join the team.

Here are some suggestions of refactoring, most of them adapted/stolen from Martin Fowler's "Refactoring - Improving the design of existing code" book.

When to refactor

The best time to refactor is right after some piece of code is written. Have a look at the code you just written and check if you can do a better job.

You can refactor as well when you add a new functionality. Maybe the old code was awesome. Maybe the new code you added is excellent. But when put together, new changes might be needed. Just like when redecorating a room of the house, the hallway might need a coat of paint, so a new piece of code might trigger refactoring for the old one.

When a bug is investigated and fixed, better way of writing related code might become apparent. Do not lose the opportunity to refactor when you are fixing a problem, even if it is not required in order to solve the problem.

And lastly, we should refactor when the code "smells bad". But let's talk about this in more details after we talk about when not to refactor.

When not to refactor

While refactoring is good, it sometimes reduces the performance so careful attention should be paid to when refactoring should be implemented and when not.

More often than not, when refactoring is done without great care it introduces new bugs.

When fixing a critical production issue, the main focus should be on solving the problem and not cleaning the code risking introducing other problems.

Refactoring should never be done when we are not sure what are we doing. If you find a piece of code that is very complicated and ugly, a chance is that there is a reason for it. Most of the time when we say about somebody else's code "What a piece of junk. I can do this in half the number of lines." there is a big chance that we are not aware of all the requirements and we are missing some important aspects.

Bad smells in the code

Kent Beck and Martin Fowler described the need for refactoring in terms of smells. To quote them: "If it stinks, change it".

It seems Kent had a newborn daughter at the time, so that explains everything.

As there are many different situations when the code "stinks", Martin lists them in his "Refactoring" book.

Here is a list adapted and added for iOS and Swift world.

Duplicated code

Functionality should be implemented only once so at any sign of duplicated code; a quick refactoring should be applied to eliminate the duplication.

Large method

Each method should have a limited size, not bigger than one screen, let's say. But more important than that, one method should do one thing and delegate all the other functionality to other methods.

Large class

Just like methods, a class should not be too large. It is not easy to define an optimal size; a class should have only one aim of existence. If it has more than that, it needs to be split.

Long parameter list

One method should have a limited number of parameters. Ideally is to receive none and to use the properties of the class it is part of. One or two parameters are okay. More than that asks for trouble.

Divergent change

When making a change, the code should be modified just in one area. If for each change, code needs to be modified in separate areas or even separate classes, some refactoring is due.

Feature Envy

This appears when one class uses too much of the attributes or methods of other class. If that is the case, maybe the methods should be moved into the first class.

Switch or if-else statements

Where there are too much branched code and in many different places, the class needs to be refactored and different functionality dealt by subclassing.

Lazy class

A lazy class is a class that is not doing much and it is not justifying its existence. In that case, it needs to be eliminated and its functionality move somewhere else.

Message chains

If to work, a class A needs some information from class B that asks C that asks D, then something is not right. Maybe A should ask directly D.

Inappropriate Intimacy

Just like people, classes should not inspect too much other classes' private parts (that is properties, some functions, etc.). When that is the case, the intruder needs to behave and mind its own business.

Comments

Comments can be stinky in so many ways: they are missing, they are too many, they exist but are confusing. Funny comments might be funny but not useful. See the chapter about comments.

Confusing names for methods or classes

When a name does not totally explain its owner reason to exist, a new name needs to be chosen. Adding a comment for a name does not solve the problem.

Not used code, parameter, class etc.

Sometimes functionality is forgotten about and never used. It is time to go.

Ugly code

The code needs to be beautiful as programming is an art (at least so the programmers believe). Code can be ugly because the code standards are not respected (or do not exist), naming is inconsistent, the logic is too complex, etc. If so, it needs to be "beautified".

How to refactor

There are many areas where refactoring can be applied. We divided them into refactoring for methods, class fields, classes, variables, conditionals, and code in general.

While some of the refactoring activities bring obvious benefit, some are a matter of preference. Feel free to adapt the methods presented to your own style.

Refactoring Methods

Extract method

The simplest method of refactoring and maybe the most used is performed by moving the code around.

We can move it from one function to another, from one class to another or create a new entity, in our case, a new function.

Consider the following function to validate three fields: first name, last name and address. Each variable has to contain a non-empty string.

```
var firstName, lastName, address : String?

firstName = "John"
lastName = "Smith"
address = "20 New Way St."

func validateForm() -> Bool {
    var valid = true

    if (firstName == nil)
       || (firstName!.count == 0) {
        valid = false
    }
    if (lastName == nil)
       || (lastName!.count == 0) {
        valid = false
    }
    if (address == nil)
       || (lastName!.count == 0) {
        valid = false
    }
    return valid
}
```

While the code is just fine for a short method, what if there are more fields? Also, what if the rule changes, for example each item should have at least two characters?

We easily notice that the same code is repeated. This was probably done by copy paste. What we might not have noticed is that we have a bug:

```
if (address == nil) || (lastName!.count == 0) {
    valid = false
}
```

I am sure this happened to you too when programming by "copy/paste".

We'll extract the duplicated code as a separate method:

```
func validateItem(item: String?) -> Bool {
    if (item == nil) || (item!.count == 0) {
        return false
    }
    return true
}
```

Our method becomes:

```
func validateForm() -> Bool {
    var valid = true

    if !validateItem(firstName) {
        valid = false
    }
    if !validateItem(lastName) {
        valid = false
    }
    if !validateItem(address) {
        valid = false
    }
    return valid
}
```

Assuming the validation rules change and the minimum length for each item is two, we need to change just `validateItem` method:

```
func validateItem(item: String?) -> Bool{
    if (item == nil) || (item!.count < 2) {
        return false
    }
    return true
}
```

Inline method

Refactoring by inline method is the opposite of the Extract method we've just analyzed.

In this case, a method is so short and it is used only in one or two spots that is it not worth having it separately.

This refactoring is done by removing the method and replacing each call with its content.

Consider the following piece of code:

```
var name: String?
name = "John"

func checkNameIsPresent() -> Bool {
    if (name == nil) || (name!.count == 0) {
        return false
    }
    return true
}

func doSomething() {
    //some code
    if !checkNameIsPresent() {
        print("Please enter your name first")
    }
    //some other code
}
```

In this case we can replace the code with the following one:

```
func doSomethingBetter() {
    //some code
    if (name == nil) || (name!.count == 0) {
        print("Please enter your name first")
    }
    //some code
}
```

In this simple example, it might not be obvious the advantage of the second option. But imagine that checkNameIsPresent is in a different part of the class, in another class or in a parent. One developer might need to spend few minutes to discover what it does.

In the second example, it is obvious what the code does right away.

Move method

"Yesterday, I froze some water."

While this is possible (I took some water, put it in a container, and in the freezer), it sounds funny. Of course, I did not freeze the water, because I don't do that. I am not a freezer. The freezer freezes water, that is why it is called a freezer.

"As it snowed today, I will blow the snow."

I will what?!? Of course, I will use the snow blower to blow the snow. That is why it is called a snow blower because it blows the snow.

All this is obvious.

Let's see the following example:

```
class Address {
    var street = ""
    var city = ""
    var country = ""
    var postalCode = ""
}
```

```
class User {
    var address = Address()

    func createFullAddress() -> String {
        return address.street + ", " + address.city
        + " ," + address.postalCode + ", " + address.country
    }
}
```

All good? Sort of.

Why does User class need to know about how to format the address? Address needs to know how to format itself.

So, move the method over and get the following nice and refactored code:

```
class Address {
    var street = ""
    var city = ""
    var country = ""
    var postalCode = ""

    func createFullAddress() -> String {
        return street + ", " + city + " ,"
            + postalCode + ", " + country
    }
}

class User {
    var address = Address()
}
```

And if you really need to have a method in User called createFullAddress, for example when this code is part of the library, add it to the User class but delegate the functionality to the right owner, Address:

```
class User {
    var address = Address()

    func createFullAddress() -> String {
        return address.createFullAddress()
    }
}
```

Introduce new method

Consider you have a method that performs an activity on an object of a certain class in multiple places across the class and the project.

Sometimes, it makes sense to add that functionality directly to the class.

Swift makes this very simple using an extension. It allows to add new functionality to an existing class, structure or enumeration even if you do not have access to its code.

Let's take the following example:

```
class Activity {
    var durationInSeconds: Double = 0

    func durationAsMinutes() -> Double {
        return durationInSeconds/60
    }
    func durationAsHours() -> Double {
        return durationInSeconds/60/60
    }
    func durationAsDays() -> Double {
        return durationInSeconds/60/60/24
    }
}
```

The disadvantage of this code is that the functionality to convert seconds into minutes, hours and days is local to the Activity class. What if there is another class that needs the same methods? Will we replicate the code? What if there is another property in Activity (for example delayInSeconds) that needs the same functionality.

In our case, it makes sense to add this functionality directly to the type used, in this case Double.

We can create an extension in the following way:

```
extension Double {
    var minutes: Double {
        return self/60
    }
    var hours: Double {
        return self/60/60
    }
    var days: Double {
        return self/24/60/60
    }
}
```

Consider we have the following variable:

```
let duration: Double = 1200
```

We can convert it to minutes, hours and days, in the following way

```
duration.minutes
duration.hours
duration.days
```

Of course, this functionality is accessible to any other code in the current module.

Extract utility method

When working on a project, especially when multiple developers are involved, the same functionality might be duplicated in different classes.

This is not only a waste of bytes but it increases the chance of bugs and makes maintenance difficult.

The code needs to be merged and moved in the class that makes more sense or into a new class.

Consider the following two classes:

```
class User {
    func trim(s: String) -> String {
        return s.stringByTrimmingCharactersInSet(
            NSCharacterSet.whitespaceAndNewlineCharacterSet()
        )
    }
    //more functionality
}

class Product {
    func trimString(s: String) -> String {
        return s.stringByTrimmingCharactersInSet(
            NSCharacterSet.whitespaceAndNewlineCharacterSet()
        )
    }
    //more functionality
}
```

We notice that `trim` and `trimString` have the same functionality.

The first solution would be to create an utility class to include both functionality:

```
class Util {
    class func trim(s: String) -> String {
        return s.stringByTrimmingCharactersInSet(
            NSCharacterSet.whitespaceAndNewlineCharacterSet()
        )
    }
}
```

We defined it as a class method so we can simply call the method like follows:

```
Util.trim(" qqq \n\t")
```

A better solution is to create an extension to the class String:

```
extension String {
    func trim() -> String {
        return self.stringByTrimmingCharactersInSet(
            NSCharacterSet.whitespaceAndNewlineCharacterSet()
        )
    }
```

```
}
```

In this case we can simply call the trim functionality:

```
" qqq \n\t".trim()
```

Extract surrounding method

Apply this refactoring when two or more methods are identical except a piece of code somewhere in the middle.

You can create a method to contain the common code that receives a closure or a method to deal with the difference in code.

Consider we have couple of methods as follows. One is displaying the squares and the other one the cubes for values between one and ten.

```
func printSquares() {
    print("---")
    for i in 1...10 {
        print (i*i)
    }
    print("---")
}

func printCubes() {
    print("---")
    for i in 1...10 {
        print (i*i*i)
    }
    print("---")
}

printSquares()
printCubes()
```

We notice that the methods are identical, except the bold code.

We can create two methods for the difference in functionality.

```
func square(number: Int) -> Int {
    return number * number
}
```

```
func cube(number: Int) -> Int {
    return number * number * number
}
```

Our refactored method will receive a method as a parameter

```
func printExponential(f:(Int)->Int){
    print("---")
    for i in 1...10 {
        print (f(i))
    }
    print("---")
}
```

Now we can invoke our new method in the following way:

```
printExponential(square)
```

```
printExponential(cube)
```

Now our code is very flexible. If we want to obtain a list of fourth power, we just need to write another method and invoke it without writing the main code again:

```
func fourthPower(number: Int) -> Int {
    return number * number * number * number
}
```

```
printExponential(fourthPower)
```

As I mentioned we can use directly closures:

```
printExponential { (n:Int) -> Int in
    n*n*n*n
}
```

As the parameter type is known, we can simplify even more:

```
printExponential { n in
    n*n*n*n
}
```

And even more:

```
printExponential ( {$0 * $0 * $0 * $0} )
```

Extract template method

Use this refactoring method when different classes have one method that is performing the same steps but each step is different.

We can create a common method (a template method that is) in the superclass and define each step in the subclasses.

Let's consider the following example:

```
class Cube {
    var side: Float = 0

    func printDescription() {
        print("This is a cube")
        print("It has the side \(side)")
        print("It has the perimeter \(side*4)")
        print("It has the area \(side*side)")
    }
}

class Rectangle {
    var width: Float = 0
    var height: Float = 0

    func printDescription() {
        print("This is a rectangle")
        print("It has the width \(width) and height
\(height)")
        print("It has the perimeter \((width+height)*2)")
        print("It has the area \(width*height)")
    }
}
```

Here is some test code:

```
let cube = Cube()
cube.side = 5
cube.printDescription()

let rectangle = Rectangle()
```

```
rectangle.width = 3
rectangle.height = 2
rectangle.printDescription()
```

The `printDescription` method is performing similar steps (print the type of class, the sides, the perimeter and the area) but each step is different.

In the superclass, we can extract a common method that performs the individual steps but define the steps in the subclass.

```
class Shape {
    func printDescription() {
        printShapeType()
        printSides()
        printPerimeter()
        printArea()
    }
    func printShapeType() {}
    func printSides() {}
    func printPerimeter() {}
    func printArea() {}
}
```

We can now remove `printDescription` from the subclasses, but override each individual step:

```
class Cube: Shape {
    var side: Float = 0
    override func printShapeType() {
        print("This is a cube")
    }
    override func printSides() {
        print("It has the side \(side)")
    }
    override func printPerimeter() {
        print("It has the perimeter \(side*4)")
    }
    override func printArea() {
        print("It has the area \(side*side)")
    }
}

class Rectangle: Shape {
    var width: Float = 0
    var height: Float = 0
```

```
    override func printShapeType() {
        print("This is a rectangle")
    }
    override func printSides() {
        print("It has the width \(width) and height
\(height)")
    }
    override func printPerimeter() {
        print("It has the perimeter \((width+height)*2)")
    }
    override func printArea() {
        print("It has the area \(width*height)")
    }
}
```

If we have a different shape, in order to have `printDescription` working properly all we need to do is to implement each step.

Hide method

Just like human beings, the classes have some public and some private "parts". And as we know very well, the private business is better to stay private.

As a rule, it is good to make everything private to start with and only make something public if really needed.

Let's consider the following class:

```
class Account {
    func generateStatement() {
        generateStatementHeader()
        generateStatementBody()
        generateStatementFooter()
    }

    func generateStatementHeader() {
        //...
    }

    func generateStatementBody() {
        //...
    }

    func generateStatementFooter() {
```

```
        //...
    }
}
```

Among other functionality, this class has a method to generate a statement. This method is calling other three ones for generating the header, body and footer.

In this context, the methods generating parts of the statement should not be accessible from outside, so we can make them private:

```swift
class Account {
    func generateStatement() {
        generateStatementHeader()
        generateStatementBody()
        generateStatementFooter()
    }

    private func generateStatementHeader() {
        //...
    }

    private func generateStatementBody() {
        //...
    }

    private func generateStatementFooter() {
        //...
    }
}
```

This reduces the risk that another class is accessing these methods and simplifies the life of other developers that are inspecting the public API of the class without looking at the code.

Introduce named parameter

Functions in Swift allow two types of parameters: named and unnamed.

When calling the function, for the named parameters their name has to be provided. For the unnamed, just the value of the parameter is sufficient.

Sometimes it makes sense to have unnamed parameters.

For example, a function that has is calculating the maximum of two numbers can be invoked as `max (3, 7)` without causing any confusion.

Some functions have the first parameter unnamed and the rest of them named (actually this is the default setting for functions in Swift).

For example:

```
class User {
    //...
}

func calculateYearlySalaryForUser(user: User, year: Int) {
    //...
}

let user = User()

calculateYearlySalaryForUser(user: user, year: 2016)
```

This is pretty clear.

In some cases, for some unknown reasons, the developer might choose to use only unnamed parameters, like in the following example:

```
func formatAddress(_ street: String, _ number: String,
    _ city: String, _ country: String) {
    print("\(number) \(street), \(city), \(country) ")
}
```

For calling this function, we need to use the following code:

```
formatAddress("Younge St.", "1234", "Toronto", "Canada")
```

This can be a bit hard to remember and it is prone to mistakes.

The solution is to use only named parameters, like follows:

```
func formatAddress(street: String, number: String,
        city: String, country: String) {
    print("\(number) \(street), \(city), \(country) ")
}
```

In this case, calling the function has the following format:

```
formatAddress(street: "Younge St.", number: "1234",
    city: "Toronto", country: "Canada")
```

Now it is clear what each parameter is.

Parameterize method

When you have similar methods that are doing the same thing with the exception of a value, create one common method and pass the value.

Let's consider the following (ugly) class for a product:

```
class Product {
    var price: Float = 0

    func increasePriceBy5Percent() {
        price = price * 1.05
    }

    func increasePriceBy10Percent() {
        price = price * 1.1
    }

    func decreasePriceBy5Percent() {
        price = price * 0.95
    }

    func decreasePriceBy10Percent() {
        price = price * 0.9
    }
}
```

Let's create a test product and apply the methods:

```
let product = Product()
product.price = 100

product.increasePriceBy10Percent()
product.increasePriceBy5Percent()
product.decreasePriceBy10Percent()
product.decreasePriceBy5Percent()
```

We notice that the methods perform the same actions with the exception of the percentage value.

We can easily create just one method and receive the percentage as a parameter:

```
class Product {
    var price: Float = 0

    func applyPercentage(percentage:Float) {
        price = price * (1 + percentage)
    }
}
```

Our method calls become now:

```
product.applyPercentage(0.1)
product.applyPercentage(0.05)
product.applyPercentage(-0.1)
product.applyPercentage(-0.05)
```

Not only the code is cleaner, but also it allows us more freedom. For example, we can now apply an increase of 20%.

Preserve the whole object

You can use this refactoring when your code is getting few properties from an object and then pass them to a method. You can simply pass the whole object.

```
class User {
    var firstName: String
    var lastName: String
}
```

We have a method that creates the header for a report. It is using the two values like follows:

```
func createHeader(firstName: String, lastName: String) {
    //...
}
```

To use the code, we need to do the following

```
let user = User()
let firstName = user.firstName
let lastName = user.lastName

createHeader(firstName: firstName, lastName: lastName)
```

We notice that the `firstName` and `lastName` variables are just temporary ones that do not bring any value.

One first step would be to remove them in the following way:

```
let user = User()
createHeader(firstName:user.firstName,
             lastName: user.lastName)
```

But we can do even better than that. We can change the method to accept the `User` object altogether:

```
func createHeader(user: User) {
    //...
}
```

If in the future, we want to add other information to the header, for example user's phone number, the change is a piece of cake.

Remove the named parameter

The functions in Swift can have named or unnamed parameters. Usually, named parameters give more clarity on their purpose. Sometime though, the names are redundant. In those cases, the names can be removed.

For example, in the following cases:

```
func max(firstValue: Float, secondValue: Float) -> Float {

    if firstValue < secondValue {
        return secondValue
    } else {
        return firstValue
    }
}

func powerOfTwo(power: Int) -> Float {
    if power < 0 {
        return 1 / powerOfTwo(power: -power)
    }
    if power == 0 {
        return 1
    }
    return 2 * powerOfTwo(power: power-1)
}
```

We can invoke the functions as follows:

```
max(firstValue: 10, secondValue: 20)

powerOfTwo(power: 10)
```

The parameters' names are not bringing any value to the code. It is obvious that the first one is calculating the maximum between two numbers. The order of the numbers does not matter.

The second one is calculating the power of two. The parameter is the power and that is obvious.

We can remove the parameter names, making the code simpler:

```
func max(_ firstValue: Float, _ secondValue: Float) -> Float {
    if firstValue < secondValue {
        return secondValue
    } else {
        return firstValue
    }
}

func powerOfTwo(_ power: Int) -> Float {
    if power < 0 {
        return 1 / powerOfTwo(-power)
    }
    if power == 0 {
        return 1
    }
    return 2 * powerOfTwo(power-1)
}
```

In this case, we can call the functions as follows:

```
max(10, 20)
powerOfTwo(10)
```

Remove the parameter

This refactoring is so simple that we'll not even give an example to prove it.

With functionality change, some of the parameters of a function become obsolete and not used.

When that is the case, of course, they need to be removed.

Easier said than done in some cases, especially when the functions are part of a library used by other parties.

In that case, we can keep the function with the extra parameter that is not used, deprecated it, and create another function with the correct parameters.

At least the new users of the function will know to use the correct version.

Let's assume the following function:

```
func testFunction(param1: Int, param2: Int, unusedParam: Int){
}
```

After few iterations, `unusedParam` is not used anymore. We can remove it right away, but this will break few other programs that are using our function.

So instead of doing that, we can mark it as deprecated and create a new, refactored version as follows:

```
@available(*,
deprecated=1.0,
message="unusedParam is not used anymore")
func testFunction(param1: Int, param2: Int, unusedParam: Int){
    testFunction(param1: param1, param2: param2)
}

func testFunction(param1:Int, param2: Int) {
    //move here the code from the previous function
}
```

Rename method

When to rename a method or a function?

But before that, do you know what is the difference between a method and a function?

Well, a method is a married function :-).

Joking, a method is a function that is associated (for life) with another class. So, a method is a function that belongs to a class.

Back to our refactoring.

We need to rename a function in one of the following cases:

- the previous developer picked a name so bad that nobody understands what it is about. Remember the name should tell us everything we need to know about its purpose

- the purpose of the function changed

- the return type changed. For example, if `getUser` is now returning an Account, of course it needs to be changed to `getAccount`.

- the name is not following the coding standards the team adopted.

Finding a good name is not easy. But working with bad names is a pain, so the effort is paying off.

Replace parameter with method

Apply this method when the code is invoking one function and passes the result to another function.

If the second function can invoke the function by itself, it should.

Let's consider the following class:

```
class User {}
```

And a function that retrieves the current user:

```
func getCurrentUser() -> User {
    var currentUser: User
    //find the user ...
    return currentUser
}
```

The following function returns all the friends of a user:

```
func findFriendsForCurrentUser(user: User) -> [User] {
    var array = [User]()
    //uses user to find his friends
    return array
}
```

We can invoke the functionality as follows:

```
let currentUser = User()

let currentUserFriends =
    findFriendsForCurrentUser(currentUser)
```

We notice though, that we always use the functionality for the current user.

So, there is no point in passing the current user.

We remove the parameter and change the function to get the current user by itself:

```
func findFriendsForCurrentUser() -> [User] {
    let user = getCurrentUser()
    var array = [User]()
    //uses user to find his friends
    return array
}
```

Replace method with method object

This refactoring can be applied when one class uses contains functionality that is independent of the class itself. Independent functionality needs to be moved outside of the class and invoked.

Let's consider the following class:

```
class User {
        init() {
                initDatabase()
                connectToDatabase()
                getUsersFromDatabase()
                //other functionality
    }
```

```
    func initDatabase(){
        //....
    }
    func connectToDatabase(){
        //...
    }
    func getUsersFromDatabase(){
        //...
    }
}
```

The database functions can have hundreds of lines, none of them really related to the User class.

To simplify the code, we can move all the related database functions outside in another class, let's call it DatabaseManager:

```
class DatabaseManager {
    func initDatabase(){
        //....
    }
    func connectToDatabase(){
        //...
    }
    func getUsersFromDatabase(){
        //...
    }
}
```

Our User class becomes:

```
class User {
    let databaseManager = DatabaseManager()

    init() {
        databaseManager.initDatabase()
        databaseManager.connectToDatabase()
        databaseManager.getUsersFromDatabase()
        //other functionality
    }
}
```

In this way, the User does not need to know about the database and other classes are able to access the same functionality.

As a rule, one class as well as one function should do just one thing. This is called Single responsibility principle.

Encapsulate downcast

Consider the following class hierarchy:

```
class Car {
    //....
}

class ElectricCar: Car {
    //...
}
```

We have a small database of cars:

```
var cars = [Car(), Car(), ElectricCar(), ElectricCar(), Car()]
```

And one function that is returning one electric car:

```
func findElectricCar() -> Car? {
    for car in cars {
        if car is ElectricCar {
            return car
        }
    }
    return nil
}
```

For the sake of argument, ignore the fact that the function is always returning the same object.

In our code, in multiple places we have to downcast the objects from Car to ElectricCar:

```
var electricCar1, electricCar2, electricCar3: ElectricCar

electricCar1 = findElectricCar() as! ElectricCar
electricCar2 = findElectricCar() as! ElectricCar
electricCar3 = findElectricCar() as! ElectricCar
```

This, of course, is useless as we know already `findElectricCar` is returning an `Electric` car.

To improve the code, we need to move the casting directly into the function

```
func findElectricCar() -> ElectricCar? {
    for car in cars {
        if car is ElectricCar {
            return (car as! ElectricCar)
        }
    }
    return nil
}
```

Now our code looks more elegant:

```
var electricCar1, electricCar2, electricCar3: ElectricCar

electricCar1 = findElectricCar()
electricCar2 = findElectricCar()
electricCar3 = findElectricCar()
```

Refactoring Class fields

Move field

Imagine classes as families. They should hold inside only what makes sense.

One does not invite neighbors to live with him, does he? Invite them to visit, maybe, but move in, no way!

So are classes. They should hold only the fields that make sense.

Think of this absurd example:

```
class Address {
    var street = ""
    var city = ""
    var country = ""
}

class User {
    var address = Address()
    var postalCode = ""
}
```

It is obvious that postalCode should not be in User class but in Address.

I'll not insist on this, as it is too obvious.

Next time you write a class, ask about each and every field:

Should this be here?

Does this class need to know about it?

Eagerly initialized attribute

A Fibonacci sequence has each element equal to the sum of the previous two elements.

The first two elements are 1 and 1 so the sequence shows like this:

1, 1, 2, 3, 5, 8, etc.

Asked to implement a function to return one element of the series, a smarty pants developer thought to save some time at the initialization of the program and to use a lazy initialized variable:

```
var fibonacci = [Int]()
fibonacci.append(1)
fibonacci.append(1)

func getFibonacci(index:Int) -> Int {
    if index >= fibonacci.count {
        for i in fibonacci.count ... index {
            fibonacci.append(fibonacci[i-1] + fibonacci[i-2])
        }
    }
    return fibonacci[index]
}
```

This is interesting, but not very straightforward. One needs to spend few thinking cycles to understand what is happening.

The developer realizes that in the current context, only the first 50 elements in the sequence are used.

So, he is simplifying the code by initializing the elements just from the start:

```
var fibonacci = [Int]()
fibonacci.append(1)
fibonacci.append(1)

for i in 2...50 {
    fibonacci.append(fibonacci[i-1] + fibonacci[i-2])
}
```

We can even of further and simplify the code a bit further, taking advantage of the Swift shortcut of initializing an array:

```
var fibonacci = [1,1]

for i in 2...50 {
    fibonacci.append(fibonacci[i-1] + fibonacci[i-2])
}
```

Way simpler and shorter.

Pull up field

This is a simple refactoring applied when there are two subclasses with a common field. Take the field and move it to the parent class.

Consider the following class structure:

```
class BankAccount {
}

class CheckingAccount: BankAccount {
    var balance: Float = 0
}

class SavingAccount: BankAccount {
    var balance: Float = 0
}
```

The common `balance` field can be moved to the parent:

```
class BankAccount {
    var balance: Float = 0
}

class CheckingAccount: BankAccount {
}

class SavingAccount: BankAccount {
}
```

This is less code to write and some common functionality can be also moved up.

The purpose of this refactoring is to have as little duplication as possible.

Hide field

In Swift, they are three levels of access levels:
- `private`
- `internal`
- `public`

We'll ignore `fileprivate` to simplify our discussion.

Private and public are obvious. Internal access means public access for the current module, but private for everything else.

The default is the internal access, which means public if we are working with just one module.

Of course, that is not a good idea. Every class should try to hide as much as it can from the other classes.

One way to achieve this is to make everything private to start with and only change it if need be.

Here is the class used in the previous post with a bit of functionality added:

```
class Account {
    var isCheckingAccount: Bool = false
    func isChecking() -> Bool {
        return isCheckingAccount
    }
}
```

We notice that `isCheckingAccount` is never accessed directly. So, we can go ahead and make it private:

```
class Account {
    private var isCheckingAccount: Bool = false
    func isChecking() -> Bool {
        return isCheckingAccount
    }
}
```

Lazy initialized attribute

Apply the type of refactoring when you have a number of objects that are initialized at the beginning of the program and that take some time to be created. This is causing some delay.

Instead of initializing them at the start, do it only when they are needed.

Let's consider the following example.

We have an object called SlowClass that takes some time to be created.

```
class SlowClass {
    init(index: Int){
        //this takes a long time
    }
}
```

We also have a repository that needs 1000 instances of this object

```
class Repository {
    var array = [SlowClass]()
    init(){
        for i in 0...1000 {
            let slowClass = SlowClass(index: i)
            array.append(slowClass)
        }
    }
}
```

If the class takes 1/10 sec to be created, then our program will take 1.5 minutes to start. This is not acceptable.

We need to change the strategy and create the objects only for when they are needed.

One way of doing it is by changing the structure from an Array to a Dictionary:

```
class Repository {
    var dictionary = [Int:SlowClass]()

    func getSlowClassAt(index: Int) -> SlowClass {
        let slowClass = dictionary[index]
        if let slowClass = slowClass {
            return slowClass
        }
        let newSlowClass = SlowClass(index: index)
        dictionary[index] = newSlowClass
        return newSlowClass
    }
}
```

As you can see, when the program starts, the dictionary is empty.

Only when one instance is needed and it does not exist yet, it is created.

Refactoring Classes

Extract Class

According to the Single Responsibility Principle, one class should do one thing. Also, it needs to know the least amount of information to do its job.

In time though, all the classes evolve by accumulating more and more properties and functions. That is why refactoring is needed to simplify them.

One of the methods is the extract class method. When a class becomes too big, extract part of it as another class.

Consider the following User class:

```
class User {
    var firstName, lastName: String?
    var streetName, streetNumber, city, postalCode,
      country: String?

    func formatAddress() -> String {
        var formattedAddress = ""
        //create a nice formatted address, taking into
        //consideration that each of the variables can be nil
        return formattedAddress
    }
}
```

As it is a simple class, it is fine as it is.

A new request comes to have the work address added, so the first version would be:

```
class User {
    var firstName, lastName: String?
    var homeStreetName, homeStreetNumber, homeCity,
            homePostalCode, homeCountry: String?
    var workStreetName, workStreetNumber, workCity,
            workPostalCode, workCountry: String?

    func homeFormatAddress() -> String {
        var formattedAddress = ""
        //create a nicely formatted address
        return formattedAddress
    }
    func workFormatAddress() -> String {
        var formattedAddress = ""
        //create a nicely formatted address
        return formattedAddress
    }
}
```

As this might be still fine, what if the user has two work addresses?

Also, what if we need more functionality for the address: check if it is valid, display it on the map, find the distance, etc.

It is clear that the User class does not need to know all details about it.

A good solution would be to extract a new class called Address:

```
class User {
    var firstName, lastName: String?
    var homeAddress = Address()
    var workAddress = Address()

    func homeFormatAddress() -> String {
        return homeAddress.formatAddress()
    }
    func workFormatAddress() -> String {
        return workAddress.formatAddress()
    }
}
```

```
class Address {
    var streetName, streetNumber, city, postalCode,
        country: String?

    func formatAddress() -> String {
        var formattedAddress = ""
        //create a nicely formatted address
        return formattedAddress
    }
}
```

Assuming that we want to add more functionality for each address, we only need to change one class.

Inline Class

This method of refactoring is just the opposite of Extract class.

Think of a class that became so small and so unused that it does not justify its existence.

Consider following classes:

```
class User {
    var firstName, lastName: String?
    var homeAddress = Address()
...
}

class Address {
    var streetName, streetNumber, city, postalCode,
      country: String?
    var email: String?
...
}
```

Because all the users are now working virtual, keeping the physical address is not needed so our Address class becomes:

```
class Address {
    var email: String?
}
```

Such a class does not deserve to live, so we can remove it from the face of the earth and move its only property, email, into the User class:

```
class User {
    var firstName, lastName, email: String?
...
}
```

Replace Array with an Object

This refactoring applies to the case when different kinds of information are stored in an array.

For example, we have an array storing the first name, the last name and the age as follows:

```
let database = [
        "John", "Williams", "30",
        "Robert", "Jones", "40",
        "Julia", "Adams", 21]
```

While this is okay for small programs, it becomes difficult to manage for bigger databases. What is the meaning of database[234] for example? It is a first name, a last name?

We can solve this problem by having a new class, for each group of information. For example:

```
class Person {
    var firstName, lastName, age: String

    init(firstName: String, lastName: String, age: String){
        self.firstName = firstName
        self.lastName = lastName
        self.age = age
    }
}
```

In this case our database becomes:

```
let database = [
    Person(firstName: "John", lastName: "Williams", age: "30"),
    Person(firstName: "Robert", lastName: "Jones", age: "40"),
    Person(firstName: "Julia", lastName: "Adams", age: "21") ]
```

We now know that all the array elements are of the `Person` type, so the confusion about the type of an element disappeared.

And, of course, if a new type of data is added, the solution is simply just adding a new property to the class and changing the code populating the object.

Change unidirectional association to bidirectional

Many times, when coding, we use different data structures: stacks, queues, trees.

These structures have the elements linked between them, allowing parsing and searching.

Usually when we start coding such a structure we consider a unidirectional link between the elements, mostly to save memory.

Let's consider the following class:

```
class Person {
    var name: String?
    var kids = [Person] ()

    func description() -> String {
        return "Person: name = \(name)"
    }
}
```

Now, let's initialize few objects.

The name of the objects is totally against the rules we discussed in the naming chapter, but we would not call ourselves real deal programmers if we did not break some rules now and then.

```
let john = Person()
john.name = "John"

let jimmy = Person()
jimmy.name = "Jimmy"

let mary = Person()
mary.name = "Mary"
```

Let's now create an array of all the persons involved:

```
let personArray = [john, jimmy, mary]
```

And also, let's add some family ties:

```
john.kids = [jimmy, mary]
```

Now, our task is to create a function to find the parent of a person, if any. And here is the code:

```
func findParent(person: Person) -> Person? {
    for aPerson in personArray {
        for kid in aPerson.kids {
            if kid === person {
                return aPerson
            }
        }
    }
    return nil
}
```

And here is the code testing it:

```
if let parent = findParent(mary) {
    print(parent.description())
}
```

All is good in this case. We have only three people so the result is instantaneous.

In real life, we can have thousands of records maybe millions.

Imagine a database with one million people. Let's compute the time it takes to find out the list of people with parents.

For each person, we have to check all the other one million people (of course, we need to check 999 999, but let's ignore that small detail).

Also, let's assume we have a 2.5 GHz processor and that it takes ten cycles to check if two persons are the same. This is not true, but just for the sake of calculation let's assume that.

The duration will be:

1 000 000 persons x 1 000 000 persons x 10 cycles / 2 500 000 000 cycles/sec = 4000 sec = over 1h

This is not acceptable.

And here comes our refactoring trick.

Instead of a unidirectional association we can introduce a bidirectional one, just by adding another property:

```
class Person1 {
    var name: String?
    var kids = [Person] ()
    var parent: Person?
}
```

In this case, finding the parents of all the persons will take:

1 000 000 persons x 10 cycles / 2 500 000 000 cycles/sec = 1 / 250 sec = 0.004 sec

We would need to change the code that initialize the database by making sure each person object has the parent property set, if we have this information.

```
class Person {
    var name: String?
    var kids = [Person] ()
    var parent: Person?

    func description() -> String {
        return "Person: name = \(name)"
    }
}

let john = Person()
john.name = "John"

let jimmy = Person()
jimmy.name = "Jimmy"
jimmy.parent = john

let mary = Person()
mary.name = "Mary"
mary.parent = john

john.kids = [jimmy,mary]
```

Now, the function findParent does not make sense. We just need to access mary.parent to find out her parent.

Change bidirectional association to unidirectional

In the previous refactoring method, we analyzed how, sometime, adding another association between the objects can drastically improve performance and reduce the amount of code we need to write.

The situation can happen in reverse as well.

Consider the following example:

```
class Person {
    var name: String?
    var address: Address?
}
```

```
class Address {
    var streetName: String?
    //other properties

    var personArray = [Person]()
}
```

The structure of the classes is clear. For each person, we are interested in the `Address`, among other information.

There can be the case where multiple people are living at the same location, so the `Address` class has an array of `Person` objects.

What if our program is never interested in who is living at a certain address? What if only the `Person` objects are of interest and now and then the address is retrieved for a certain person?

In this case, we can safely remove the double association, save some memory and simplify the code in the process:

```
class Address {
    var streetName: String?
    //other properties
    var personArray = [Person]()
}
```

Collapse hierarchy

If a hierarchy of classes gets simplified over time, eventually it becomes so simple, that is not really needed. Then, it is time to collapse some classes.

Let's consider the following hierarchy:

```
class Car {
}

class RegularCar: Car {
}

class HybridCar: Car {
```

```
}
```

The government, in his wisdom, releases a new law to allow only hybrid cars in the market so our hierarchy becomes:

```
class Car {
}

class HybridCar: Car {
}
```

This is not useful anymore, so we can simply remove HybridCar and move all the functionality to the superclass, Car.

Replace Type Code with Polymorphism

This type of refactoring applies when a class has a property that represent a type of some kind and the code is depending on it. This usually manifests through if/else or switch statements.

We'll now dive into the martial arts domain where one practitioner (a karateka) is awarded certain belts for mastering certain elements.

For now, let's assume the belts are of three kinds: white, blue and black. They correspond to a beginner, intermediate and, respectively, advanced level.

First, we define an enumeration with the three belts:

```
enum Belt {
    case white, blue, black
}
```

Then, we'll define the Karateka class that has two methods for displaying the title and the level:

```
class Karateka {
    var belt = Belt.white
```

```
    func getTitle() -> String {
        switch belt {
        case .white :
            return "White belt karateka"
        case .blue :
            return "Blue belt karateka"
        case .black :
            return "Black belt karateka"
        }
    }

    func getLevel() -> String {
        switch belt {
        case .white :
            return "Beginner karateka"
        case .blue :
            return "Intermediate karateka"
        case .black :
            return "Advanced karateka"
        }
    }
}
```

Here is some code to test the class:

```
let karateka1 = Karateka()
karateka1.belt = .white

let karateka2 = Karateka()
karateka2.belt = .blue

let karateka3 = Karateka()
karateka3.belt = .black

karateka1.getTitle()
karateka2.getTitle()
karateka3.getTitle()

karateka1.getLevel()
karateka2.getLevel()
karateka3.getLevel()
```

The switch statements need to be replicated for each piece of functionality that depends on the belt color. Also, if one more belt is added, all the switch statements need to be changed.

Instead of this, we'll create a base class and for each belt and we'll overwrite the methods that depend on the belt type property.

```
class Karateka {
    var belt: Belt

    init() {
        belt = .white
    }

    func getTitle() -> String {
        return "unknown"
    }

    func getLevel() -> String {
        return "unknown"
    }
}
```

Now let's implement one class for each belt:

```
class KaratekaWhiteBelt: Karateka {
    override init() {
        super.init()
        super.belt = .white
    }

    override func getTitle() -> String {
        return "White belt karateka"
    }

    override func getLevel() -> String {
        return "Beginner karateka"
    }
}

class KaratekaBlueBelt: Karateka {
    override init() {
        super.init()
        super.belt = .blue
    }

    override func getTitle() -> String {
        return "Blue belt karateka"
    }

    override func getLevel() -> String {
        return "Intermediate karateka"
    }
}
```

```
class KaratekaBlackBelt: Karateka {
    override init() {
        super.init()
        super.belt = .black
    }

    override func getTitle() -> String {
        return "Black belt karateka"
    }

    override func getLevel() -> String {
        return "Advanced karateka"
    }
}
```

And here is some code to test our new refactored functionality:

```
let karateka1 = KaratekaWhiteBelt()
let karateka2 = KaratekaBlueBelt()
let karateka3 = KaratekaBlackBelt()

karateka1.getTitle()
karateka2.getTitle()
karateka3.getTitle()

karateka1.getLevel()
karateka2.getLevel()
karateka3.getLevel()
```

Code looks more elegant right now.

If we need to add more belts, all we have to do is add more subclasses and, of course, update the Belt enumeration.

All the other code stays the same.

Extract protocol

A protocol (also called interface in other languages) defines a blueprint of properties, functions and other functionality a class needs to follow.

It is used to define a certain type of classes.

Sometimes classes evolve and only after a while their common functionality becomes apparent.

Consider the following classes:

```
class Car {
    var make: String?
    var model: String?
    var mileage: Float?
    var numberOfDoors: Int?
    var maximumSpeed: Float?
    var horsePower: Float?
    var colour: UIColor?
}

class Motorcycle {
    var make: String?
    var model: String?
    var mileage: Float?
    var maximumSpeed: Float?
    var horsePower: Float?
    var colour: UIColor?
    var wheels: Int?
}
```

Because they are different classes, functionality that applies to both is difficult to write. For example, it is not easy to create an array of both cars and motorcycles and sort them by maximum speed.

We notice they have common functionality so we can extract a protocol containing it:

```
protocol Vehicle {
    var make: String? { get set }
    var model: String? { get set }
    var mileage: Float? { get set }
    var maximumSpeed: Float? { get set }
    var horsePower: Float? { get set }
    var colour: UIColor? { get set }
}
```

In this case, our classes will become:

```
class Car: Vehicle {
    var make: String?
    var model: String?
    var mileage: Float?
    var numberOfDoors: Int?
    var maximumSpeed: Float?
    var horsePower: Float?
    var colour: UIColor?
}

class Motorcycle: Vehicle {
    var make: String?
    var model: String?
    var mileage: Float?
    var maximumSpeed: Float?
    var horsePower: Float?
    var colour: UIColor?
    var wheels: Int?
}
```

A sorting function is now obvious:

```
func sortVehicle(vehicleArray:[Vehicle]) -> [Vehicle] {
    return vehicleArray.sort
    ({ $0.maximumSpeed < $1.maximumSpeed })
}
```

Here is some code to test it:

```
let v1 = Car()
v1.maximumSpeed = 100
let v2 = Motorcycle()
v2.maximumSpeed = 150
let v3 = Car()
v3.maximumSpeed = 140

var array1: [Vehicle]
array1 = [v1, v2, v3]

let array2 = sortVehicle(array1)
```

Extract subclass

In some instances, one class is providing functionality for only certain cases.

Assume there is a class to manage a bank account.

The class provides functionality for checking as well as for saving accounts but only the saving accounts bring interest to the owner.

```
class Account {
    //this function is called only for saving accounts
    func calculateInterest(){
        //....
    }
}

let checkingAccount = Account()
let savingAccount = Account()
```

Nothing prevents a user for calling `checkingAccount.calculateInterest()` and also get a result that might not be accurate or in the best case is zero.

The solution to prevent this is to create a sub class and move the specific functionality there:

```
class Account {
    //some functionality
}

class SavingAccount: Account {
    func calculateInterest(){
        //...
    }
}

let checkingAccount = Account()
let savingAccount = SavingAccount()
```

In this case, `checkingAccount.calculateInterest()` would raise a compilation error.

In general, each class should only have the functionality that allows performing its duties and nothing more.

Extract superclass

This refactoring is applied when different classes have similar functionality. In this case, the common code can be moved into a new class that becomes the superclass for the other classes.

Consider a checking and a saving account:

```
class SavingAccount {
    func calculateInterest(){
    }

    func createStatement() {
    }

    func emailStatement(){
    }
}

class CheckingAccount {
    func calculateFee(){
    }

    func createStatement() {
    }

    func emailStatement(){
    }
}
```

While the classes are not identical, we notice some common functionality.

We'll create another class, Account and extend the current class from it.

```
class Account {
    func createStatement() {
    }

    func emailStatement(){
    }
}

class SavingAccount: Account {
    func calculateInterest(){
```

```
    }
}

class CheckingAccount: Account {
    func calculateFee(){
    }
}
```

This makes the hierarchy more elegant and allows a simpler maintenance. Imagine if the emailStatement functionality needs to be changed, in our second example, we need to change it only in one place.

Introduce Null object

Objects in our programs can have null values (nil in Swift).

The functionality is different if we know the value for those objects or not, so we need to check in multiple places for that.

Let's consider the following code:

```
class Address {
    var street: String = ""
    var city: String = ""

    func formattedAddress() -> String {
        return "\(street), \(city)"
    }
}

class User {
    var address: Address?
}

let user = User()
```

Suppose in different places in the code you need information about the value of the street for a user, for example, for displaying reasons.

```
var street: String
```

```
if let address = user.address {
    street = address.street
} else {
    street = ""
}
```

Also in other places you need the city, so you have the following code:

```
var city: String
if let address = user.address {
    city = address.city
} else {
    city = ""
}
```

And so forth. This might be cumbersome and also prone to error. It is easy to forget to check for nil in one place.

The solution to this is to create one new class to include all the functionality we need to have when the address is not known.

Here is an example:

```
class NullAddress: Address {
    override init() {
        street  = ""
        city  = ""
    }

    override func formattedAddress() -> String {
        return "unknown address"
    }
}
```

And here is how our User class will look now.

```
class User {
    var address: Address = NullAddress()
}
```

So, the following code:

```
var street: String

if let address = user.address {
    street = address.street
} else {
    street = ""
}
```

will become:

```
var street = user.address.street
```

Notice the `formattedAddress()` function. If the address is unknown, it will return "unknown address" so custom functionality can also be added to our null class.

Pull up constructor body

As a rule of thumb, each time you see the same code in different places, look for ways to remove the duplication.

This refactoring applies when two or more subclasses have similar code in the `init` method. We can move that code in the superclass.

Have a look at the following example:

```
class Vehicle {
    var make: String?
    var model: String?
    var mileage: Float?
    var maximumSpeed: Float?
    var horsePower: Float?
    var colour: UIColor?

    init() {
        //...
    }
}

class Car: Vehicle {
    var numberOfDoors: Int?
```

```
    init(make: String, model: String, mileage: Float,
        maximumSpeed: Float, horsePower: Float,
        colour: UIColor, numberOfDoors: Int) {
        super.init()
        self.make = make
        self.model = model
        self.mileage = mileage
        self.maximumSpeed = maximumSpeed
        self.horsePower = horsePower
        self.colour = colour
        self.numberOfDoors = numberOfDoors
    }
}

class Motorcicle: Vehicle {
    var numberOfWheels: Int?

    init(make: String, model: String, mileage: Float,
        maximumSpeed: Float, horsePower: Float,
        colour: UIColor, numberOfWheels: Int) {
        super.init()
        self.make = make
        self.model = model
        self.mileage = mileage
        self.maximumSpeed = maximumSpeed
        self.horsePower = horsePower
        self.colour = colour
        self.numberOfWheels = numberOfWheels
    }
}
```

I marked in bold the duplicated code. To apply this refactoring, we move the common code into the superclass, removing a good few lines of code:

```
class Vehicle {
    var make: String?
    var model: String?
    var mileage: Float?
    var maximumSpeed: Float?
    var horsePower: Float?
    var colour: UIColor?

    init(make: String, model: String, mileage: Float,
        maximumSpeed: Float, horsePower: Float,
        colour: UIColor) {
        self.make = make
        self.model = model
        self.mileage = mileage
```

```
            self.maximumSpeed = maximumSpeed
            self.horsePower = horsePower
            self.colour = colour
    }
}

class Car: Vehicle {
    var numberOfDoors: Int?

    init(make: String, model: String, mileage: Float,
            maximumSpeed: Float, horsePower: Float,
            colour: UIColor, numberOfDoors: Int) {

        super.init(make: make, model: model, mileage: mileage,
            maximumSpeed: maximumSpeed, horsePower: horsePower,
            colour: colour)

        self.numberOfDoors = numberOfDoors
    }
}

class Motorcicle: Vehicle {
    var numberOfWheels: Int?

    init(make: String, model: String, mileage: Float,
      maximumSpeed: Float, horsePower: Float, colour: UIColor,
      numberOfWheels: Int) {

        super.init(make: make, model: model, mileage: mileage,
            maximumSpeed: maximumSpeed, horsePower: horsePower,
            colour: colour)
        self.numberOfWheels = numberOfWheels
    }
}
```

Pull up method

This refactoring is applied when two classes have an identical method. It can be moved up to the parent.

Consider the following example:

```
class BankAccount {
    var balance : Float = 0
}
```

```
class CheckingAccount: BankAccount {
    func displayAlert(){
        if balance < 0 {
            print("You have a negative balance of
\(balance).")
        }
    }
}

class SavingAccount: BankAccount {
    func displayAlert(){
        if balance < 0 {
            print("You have a negative balance of
\(balance).")
        }
    }
}
```

We noticed we have a method (`displayAlert`) that is identical. We can move it up the hierarchy.

```
class BankAccount {
    var balance: Float = 0

    func displayAlert(){
        if balance < 0 {
            print("You have a negative balance of \(balance).")
        }
    }
}

class CheckingAccount: BankAccount {
}

class SavingAccount: BankAccount {
}
```

Push down field or method

This refactoring is applied when there is a field or method in a superclass that is used only in one of the subclasses.

One class should have the information it needs to have, so it makes sense to push down that field or method to the subclass where it belongs.

Here is an example:

```
class BankAccount {
    var overdraft: Float = 0

    func enableOverdraft(overdraft: Float){
    }
}

class CheckingAccount: BankAccount {
}

class SavingAccount: BankAccount {
}
```

BankAccount has the overdraft, but, according to the business rules, an overdraft applies only to a checking account. In this case we can move the functionality to the CheckingAccount class.

```
class BankAccount {
}

class CheckingAccount: BankAccount {
  var overdraft: Float = 0

    func enableOverdraft(overdraft: Float){
    }
}

class SavingAccount: BankAccount {
}
```

By doing this, not only we move the functionality to the place where it belongs, but we also eliminate the risk to have this functionality called for the incorrect object.

For example, in the first case, the overdraft functionality could have been called for a saving account, which is incorrect.

Replace subclass with fields

The subclasses need to have a reason for existence; a very good reason.

When that reason disappears or becomes slim, it might be time for removing the subclass.

Let's consider the following hierarchy of classes:

```
class Account {
    func isChecking() -> Bool {
        return false
    }
}

class CheckingAccount: Account {
    override func isChecking() -> Bool {
        return true
    }
}

class SavingAccount: Account {
    override func isChecking() -> Bool {
        return false
    }
}
```

While at the beginning the `CheckingAccount` and `SavingAccount` were different in functionality, in time, the only difference between them remained just the `isChecking` method that returns `true` for one and `false` for another.

We can refactor this structure, by adding one property to the `Account` class to reflect if the account is checking or not.

```
class Account {
    var isCheckingAccount = false
    func isChecking() -> Bool {
        return isCheckingAccount
    }
}
```

Refactoring Variables

Introduce explaining variable

Let's build a game, or at least a very small part of the game.

```
let myShipFrame = CGRect(x: 0, y: 0, width: 100, height: 100)
let enemyShipFrame = CGRect(x: 50, y: 50, width: 100, height: 100)

if  abs((myShipFrame.origin.x + myShipFrame.width/2.0) -
        (enemyShipFrame.origin.x + enemyShipFrame.width/2.0)) <
        (myShipFrame.width/2.0 + enemyShipFrame.width/2.0) {
    gameFinished = true
}
```

Huh?!?

Exactly!

We understand that we have two ships, each of them defined as a rectangle (CGRect) and that we somehow decide if the game is finished. How that is done is not that clear.

In this situation, to make the code more obvious, we can introduce a variable that has only one purpose: to explain the code.

Let's change the above code as follows:

```
let shipCollided =
  abs((myShipFrame.origin.x + myShipFrame.width/2.0) -
  (enemyShipFrame.origin.x + enemyShipFrame.width/2.0)) <
  (myShipFrame.width/2.0 + enemyShipFrame.width/2.0)

if shipCollided {
    gameFinished = true
}
```

While the formula is still confusing, we now understand that it calculates if our ship collided. This helps a lot.

Split temporary variable

For the previous example, we can even go further. We understand what the formula is for but we do not really understand how it is calculating this fact. So, we can add few more explaining variables:

```
let myShipCenter =
      myShipFrame.origin.x + myShipFrame.width/2.0
let enemyShipCenter =
      enemyShipFrame.origin.x + enemyShipFrame.width/2.0
let minimumDistanceForCollision =
      myShipFrame.width/2.0 + enemyShipFrame.width/2.0
let shipCollided =
      abs(myShipCenter - enemyShipCenter)
        < minimumDistanceForCollision

if shipCollided {
    gameFinished = true
}
```

Without looking at the calculations we understand that the two ships collide if the distance between the centres of the ships (that is abs(myShipCenter - enemyShipCenter)) is smaller than the minimum distance for collision (minimumDistanceForCollision).

Now the code is way more obvious than the first version.

And, of course, we realize the code has a bug as it is considering only X axis and the same check needs to be done on Y axis. But that is your homework :-)

Inline temp

This refactoring is the reverse of the Explaining variable one.

You added a new variable to make the code clearer. But after few changes the variable is not really useful.

Consider the following piece of code:

```
class User {
    var isAdmin = true
    //...
}

let user = User()

var userIsAdmin = user.isAdmin

if userIsAdmin {
    //do something
}
```

It is obvious that `userIsAdmin` is not really needed. We can easily remove it and have the following code:

```
class User {
    var isAdmin = true
    //...
}

let user = User()

if user.isAdmin {
    //do something
}
```

Introduce Assertion

An **assertion** in Swift is a run time check for a particular condition to be true. If that is the case, the execution of the program continues. If not, the code execution stops and the program is terminated.

Assertions are disabled when the app is built for production, so the users will not see their app crashing.

One can use assertion for verifying a condition is fulfilled when the current implementation expects it to be always fulfilled.

Assume the program is iterating the elements of an array. One would expect that the index of the current element is always positive and less than the number of elements in the array.

Sometimes the data is depending on external factors (for example an external library) and there is a chance that it might be incorrect.

Let's consider an app that records the information about a user in the following class (we kept only the functionality needed for our example):

```
class User {
    var age = 0

    func setAge(age: Int) {
        self.age = age
    }
}
```

Our app is asking the user to input their date of birth, that needs to be before today's date, and then computes the age. In the current scenario, the age will always be positive.

What if the functionality changes in the future and the age is read from a database? From various reasons (like being corrupt data, for example), the age can be negative so the functionality of our program will not work properly.

We want to catch that issue right when it happens.

For this we can add an assert in the following way:

```
class User {
    var age = 0

    func setAge(age: Int) {
        assert(age >= 0,
        "Age is not positive. Current value is \(age)")
        self.age = age
    }
```

```
}
```

Here is some test code:

```
let user = User()
user.setAge(10)
user.setAge(-5)
```

The second time the age is set, our program will crash preventing other errors to be raised later.

Of course, one should never use asserts for all the cases. For example, if in our case the age is input by the user, he can introduce a negative one or maybe a non-numeric value. In this case, the program should validate input data is correct and display a nice message.

Asserts are only for cases when we are positive that a certain condition is fulfilled all the time.

Refactoring Conditional

Consolidate conditional expressions

This refactoring is applied when there are multiple conditional tests that have the same outcome. You can combine them in the same condition.

Consider the following piece of code that is checking if the length of a username is correct (that is between 5 and 20).

```
let username: String?

username = "test"

var lengthCorrect = true
if username == nil {
    lengthCorrect = false
} else if username?.count < 5 {
    lengthCorrect = false
} else  if username?.count > 20 {
    lengthCorrect = false
}
```

As you can see all the tests have the same outcome: length is incorrect

The first step would be to combine all the checks into the same if statement:

```
if (username == nil) || (username?.count < 5)
    || (username?.count > 20) {
    lengthCorrect = false
}
```

Of course, the next step is to extract this code into its own function:

```
func checkUsernameLength(username:String?) -> Bool {
    return !((username == nil)
             || (username?.count < 5)
             || (username?.count > 20))
}
```

Now, the code to check the validity of the username is simply:

```
var lengthCorrect = checkUsernameLength(username)
```

Consolidate Duplicate Conditional Fragments

Apply this refactoring when the same code is duplicated in the branches of an if/else or switch statement.

Move the common code outside of the statement.

Let's consider the following code that is creating the full name using the first and last name:

```
var firstName, lastName: String?

//....

var fullName = ""
if firstName == nil {
    if lastName == nil {
        fullName = "unknown name"
        print(fullName)
    } else {
        fullName = lastName!
        print(fullName)
    }
} else {
    if lastName == nil {
        fullName = firstName!
        print(fullName)
    } else {
        fullName = firstName! + " " + lastName!
        print(fullName)
    }
}
```

We can easily notice that for each branch the full name is printed.

We can move it outside the branch as follows:

```
var fullName = ""
if firstName == nil {
    if lastName == nil {
        fullName = "unknown name"
    } else {
        fullName = lastName!
    }
} else {
    if lastName == nil {
        print(fullName)
    } else {
        fullName = firstName! + " " + lastName!
    }
}
print(fullName)
```

Decompose conditional

Simple code is easier to understand and maintain. One of the aim of refactoring techniques is to be sure the code is as simple as it can be.

This refactoring can be applied in the case of a long series of conditionals. They can be too difficult to follow and easy to get wrong.

Let's write some code that is calculating the taxes one has to pay. In our example, there are 5 levels of tax, depending on the income and number of kids.

```
if (income < 1000) && (kids == 0) { //level 1
    tax = income * 0.2
} else if (income < 1000) && (kids > 0) { //level 2
    tax = income * 0.1
} else if (income < 2000) && (kids == 0) { //level 3
    tax = 200 + (income - 10000) * 0.3
} else if (income < 2000) && (kids > 0) { //level 4
    tax = 100 + (income - 1000) * 0.2
} else {
    tax = 400 + (income - 2000) * 0.4 //level 5
}
```

It is not easy to follow the code, let alone change. Imagine what would have happened if there were 20 levels instead of 5.

We can simplify it by extracting a function for each conditional and each branch:

```
if checkLevel1() {
    tax = computeTaxLevel1()
} else if checkLevel2() {
    tax = computeTaxLevel2()
} else if checkLevel3() {
    tax = computeTaxLevel3()
} else if checkLevel4() {
    tax = computeTaxLevel1()
} else {
    tax = computeTaxLevel5()
}
```

Each of the function is defined as follows:

```
func checkLevel1() -> Bool {
    return (income < 1000) && (kids == 0)
}

func computeTaxLevel1() -> Double {
    return income * 0.2
}
```

The other ones are similar.

Now the code is clear and also for changing one level, one knows exactly where to do it: in the function corresponding to that level.

Remove control flag

Sometimes when there are a series of conditional tests, we use a flag to keep a temporary Boolean value.

If this is happening inside a function we can replace this flag with return or exit statement.

Have a look at the following example:

```
class User {
    var firstName = ""
    var middleName = ""
    var lastName = ""
}
```

We also have a database of users:

```
var userArray = [User]()
```

And here is a search function for a user that has a specific name:

```
func searchName(name: String) -> User? {
    var found = false
    var user: User?

    for var index = 0; (index < userArray.count) && !found;
      ++index {

        let crtUser = userArray[index]

        if crtUser.firstName == name {
            user = crtUser
            found = true
        }

        if crtUser.middleName == name {
            user = crtUser
            found = true
        }

        if crtUser.lastName == name {
            user = crtUser
            found = true
        }
    }
    return user
}
```

So many lines for a simple search.

We can eliminate the variable and instead of storing locally the user, we can just return it as follows:

```
func searchName(name: String) -> User? {

    for var index = 0; index < userArray.count; ++index {

        let crtUser = userArray[index]

        if crtUser.firstName == name {
            return crtUser
        }

        if crtUser.middleName == name {
            return crtUser
        }

        if crtUser.lastName == name {
            return crtUser
        }
    }
    return nil
}
```

We can continue the refactoring by combining all the tests in one:

```
func searchName(name:String) -> User? {

    for var index = 0; index < userArray.count; ++index {

        let crtUser = userArray[index]

        if (crtUser.firstName == name)
            || (crtUser.middleName == name)
            || (crtUser.lastName == name) {
            return crtUser
        }
    }
    return nil
}
```

Also, we notice that a for-in might work better and the code look more elegant:

```
func searchName(name:String) -> User? {

    for crtUser in userArray {

        if (crtUser.firstName == name)
```

```
            || (crtUser.middleName == name)
            || (crtUser.lastName == name) {
               return crtUser
        }
    }
    return nil
}
```

Simplify nested conditionals with returns

Consider the case when a function needs to calculate the result using a complicated set of logic statements based on the input.

We would need to store the result in a variable and return it at the end. Or do we?

As for the previous posts, the following example is simple and is not necessary benefiting a lot from the refactoring. They are just simple examples to make the topic clearer and prove the point.

In the real-life applications, small refactoring like this can half the amount of code needed and provide a huge increase in clarity.

Let's consider a company where the bonus of the employee is calculated based on the number of kids.

Yes, this company is in a parallel universe, you are right.

```
func bonusForSalary(salary: Float, numberOfKids: Int)
                                          -> Float {
    var bonus: Float

    if numberOfKids == 0 {
        bonus = salary * 0.2
    } else if numberOfKids == 1 {
        bonus = salary * 0.3
    } else if numberOfKids == 2 {
        bonus = salary * 0.4
    } else if numberOfKids == 3 {
        bonus = salary * 0.5
    } else {
        bonus = salary * 0.6
    }
```

```
      return bonus
}
```

We notice that bonus variable is used only twice for each case, once when it is assigned and once when it is returned.

We can simplify this function by directly returning the result and removing the bonus variable:

```
func bonusForSalary(salary:Float, numberOfKids: Int)
                                        -> Float {

    if numberOfKids == 0 {
        return salary * 0.2
    }
    if numberOfKids == 1 {
        return salary * 0.3
    }
    if numberOfKids == 2 {
        return salary * 0.4
    }
    if numberOfKids == 3 {
        return salary * 0.5
    }
    return salary * 0.6
}
```

Getting rid of the code and of the variables is always a good idea when the clarity of the code is not reduced. And of course, when bugs are not added.

Refactoring Code

Replace type code with enumeration

Karate is a Japanese style of martial arts that rewards its participant attaining a certain level of sport mastery with color belts.

Let's have a class for a Karateka, that is a Karate practitioner.

```
let kWhiteBelt = 0, kYellowBelt = 1, kOrangeBelt = 3
let kGreenBelt = 4, kBlueBelt = 5, kBrownBelt = 6
let kBlackBelt = 6

class Karateka {
    var name = ""
    var belt = kWhiteBelt

    func isBeginner () -> Bool {
        return belt == kWhiteBelt
    }

    func isMaster () -> Bool {
        return belt == kBlackBelt
    }
}
```

The code works fine but it is not an elegant one.

And it is error prone. Consider the following code:

```
var belt = kYellowBelt
++belt
```

What will be the value of the belt? `kOrangeBelt`? Look again. The value of `kYellowBelt` is 1 and there is no value for 2, the current value of the belt.

Here is a more elegant solution:

```
enum Belt {
    case White, Yellow, Orange, Green, Blue, Brown, Black
}

class Karateka {
    var name = ""
    var belt = Belt.White

    func isBeginner () -> Bool {
        return belt == .White
    }

    func isMaster () -> Bool {
        return belt == .Black
    }
}
```

Trying now to use ++ operator on a Belt object will result in a compilation error.

Replace magic number with symbolic constants

Magic numbers are values with unexplained meaning and multiple occurrences in the code, according to Wikipedia. Here is an example:

```
func validateUsername(username:String?) {
    if let username = username {
        let length = username.characters.count
        if length <= 3 {
            print("Username too short.")
            print("It needs to be longer than 3.")
        } else if length >= 10 {
            print("Username too long.")
            print("It needs to be shorter than 10.")
        } else {
            print("username valid")
        }
    } else {
        print("username cannot be nil")
    }
}
```

We recognize right away the "magic numbers" as the minimum and the maximum length for a password, 3 respectively 10. We see they are present inside the error message so there is the danger that, when one of the values change, we'll forget to change the other one:

```
...
        if length <= 4 {
            print("Username too short.")
            print("It needs to be longer than 3.")
        }
...
```

So magic numbers are bad. The solution is replacing them with constants. For example:

```
let kMinimumLength = 3
let kMaximumLength = 10

func validateUsername(username:String?) {
    if let username = username {
        let length = username.characters.count
        if length <= kMinimumLength {
            print("Username too short.")
            print("It needs to be longer than
\(kMinimumLength)")
        } else if length >= kMaximumLength {
            print("Username too long.")
            print("It needs to be shorter than
\(kMaximumLength)")
        } else {
            print("username valid")
        }
    } else {
        print("username cannot be nil")
    }
}
```

If an update is needed, we need to change only the value of the constants.

The constants can be used across the class and maybe in other classes if defined as global.

We can even go further with creating the constants.

We notice that the error messages are used directly as strings. This is not a good idea as changing them might be very difficult. We can define other constants and move them also outside of the function:

```
let kMinimumLength = 3
let kMaximumLength = 10
let kUsernameTooShort = "Username too short. It needs to be
longer than \(kMinimumLength)"
let kUsernameTooLong = "Username too long. It needs to be
shorter than \(kMaximumLength)"
let kUsernameValid = "Username valid"
let kUsernameCannotBeNil = "Username cannot be nil"

func validateUsername(username:String?) {
    if let username = username {
        let length = username.characters.count
        if length <= kMinimumLength {
            print(kUsernameTooShort)
        } else if length >= kMaximumLength {
            print(kUsernameTooLong)
        } else {
            print(kUsernameValid)
        }
    } else {
        print(kUsernameCannotBeNil)
    }
}
```

Substitute algorithm

Let's continue the discussion from a previous refactoring method.

Here is the code we arrived at:

```
func bonusForSalary(salary:Float, numberOfKids: Int)
     -> Float {

    if numberOfKids == 0 {
        return salary * 0.2
    }
    if numberOfKids == 1 {
        return salary * 0.3
    }
    if numberOfKids == 2 {
        return salary * 0.4
```

```
    }
    if numberOfKids == 3 {
        return salary * 0.5
    }
    return salary * 0.6
}
```

What if there are a lot of different cases? What if we have a different percentage for 0 to 10 kids?

Also what if the bonus is different if the mother is married or not. In this case we'll have 22 different cases to analyze.

Lots of times, after few iterations, an algorithm can be recreated from start.

In this case, there are multiple solutions. Here is one:

```
func bonusForSalary(salary:Float, numberOfKids: Int)
       -> Float {

    let bonusArray:[Float] = [0.2, 0.3, 0.4, 0.5];

    if numberOfKids < bonusArray.count {
        return salary * bonusArray[numberOfKids]
    }
    return salary * 0.6
}
```

Not only the code is clearer, but also, we can very easy increase the number of cases by simply adding new values to the array.

To be continued

The book is not finished. My intention was to be a booklet 50-60 pages long. But after working on the refactoring methods, I realized it is getting too long.

So, I decided for now it is enough. For you sure you add more chapters by yourself while thinking how to improve your code.

To learn more about the topic, have a look at the books in the bibliography. Each and every one of them can change your developer life.

Bibliography

Refactoring: Improving the Design of Existing Code (Martin Fowler, Kent Beck)

Clean code - a handbook of agile software craftsmanship (Robert C. Martin)

The Clean Coder: A Code of Conduct for Professional Programmers (Robert C. Martin)

Swift Documentation (Matt Thompson & Nate Cook)
http://nshipster.com/swift-documentation

The Official raywenderlich.com Swift Style Guide
https://github.com/raywenderlich/swift-style-guide

The Art of Readable Code (Dustin Boswell and Trevor Foucher)

Rapid Development: Taming Wild Software Schedules (Steve McConnell)

The Mythical Man-Month: Essays on Software Engineering (by Frederick P. Brooks Jr.)

Code Complete: A Practical Handbook of Software Construction (Steve McConnell)

Pro Design Patterns in Swift (Adam Freeman)

Test-Driven iOS Development (Graham Lee)

www.ingramcontent.com/pod-product-compliance
Lightning Source LLC
Chambersburg PA
CBHW032023170526
45157CB00002B/827